# Times they are a-changing
## Policing of cannabis

**Tiggey May, Hamish Warburton, Paul J. Turnbull and Mike Hough**

The **Joseph Rowntree Foundation** has supported this project as part of its programme of research and innovative development projects, which it hopes will be of value to policy makers, practitioners and service users. The facts presented and views expressed in this report are, however, those of the authors and not necessarily those of the Foundation.

Mike Hough is Professor of Social Policy and Director of the Criminal Policy Research Unit at South Bank University, where Paul J. Turnbull is Deputy Director, Tiggey May is a Senior Research Fellow and Hamish Warburton is a Research Assistant.

Published for the Joseph Rowntree Foundation by YPS

ISBN 1 84263 062 8

Prepared and printed by:
York Publishing Services Ltd
64 Hallfield Road
Layerthorpe
York YO31 7ZQ
Tel: 01904 430033; Fax: 01904 430868; E-mail: orders@yps.ymn.co.uk

# Contents

|  |  | Page |
|---|---|---|
| **Acknowledgements** | | v |
| **Summary** | | vi |
| **1** | **Introduction** | 1 |
| | Background | 2 |
| | Aims and methods of the study | 3 |
| | The structure of the report | 4 |
| **2** | **Cannabis use and cannabis policing** | 5 |
| | Who uses cannabis? | 5 |
| | The cost of buying cannabis | 6 |
| | The 'normalisation' of cannabis use | 6 |
| | The Misuse of Drugs Act 1971 | 7 |
| | Policing of cannabis offences: police force policy | 8 |
| | Recent proposals for change | 10 |
| | The United Nations Conventions | 12 |
| | European approaches to cannabis possession | 12 |
| **3** | **Enforcement of the law** | 14 |
| | People coming to police attention for cannabis possession | 14 |
| | Who gets caught for cannabis possession? | 15 |
| | How cannabis possession offences come to light | 15 |
| | Possession arrests as a by-product of investigation of other offences | 15 |
| | Obvious evidence of cannabis use | 23 |
| | Cannabis possession arrests as part of an intended strategy or tactic | 24 |
| **4** | **Case disposals for cannabis possession** | 26 |
| | Informal warning or arrest? | 26 |
| | Caution or charge? | 30 |
| | Court disposals for cannabis possession | 31 |
| **5** | **Dealing with possession: costs and benefits** | 32 |
| | Social costs of policing cannabis | 32 |
| | Financial costs of policing cannabis | 36 |
| | Possible benefits | 38 |
| | Costs and benefits of the reclassification of cannabis | 41 |

**6    Discussion and conclusions**                                        44
    Key points                                         44
    Putting police time to better use                  46
    Redeploying the saved resources                    47
    Improvements in police–public relations            48
    Stigmatisation and the curtailing of life opportunities   48
    Costs in losing arrest powers                      48
    Warnings and repeat offending                      49
    Deterrence and levels of use                       49
    Cultivation and supply – choices for policy        50
    The law of unintended consequences                 51

**Notes**                                                                  52

**Bibliography**                                                           54

**Appendix 1: Methodology**                                                57

**Appendix 2: The rules that govern stop and search powers**               60

**Appendix 3: Glossary of terms**                                          61

# Acknowledgements

We owe an enormous debt of gratitude to our funders, the Joseph Rowntree Foundation. Without their generosity this study would not have been possible. In a study of this nature, however, particular thanks are due to the operational police officers who explained the intricacies and idiosyncrasies of policing with humour, patience and honesty over the course of many long night shifts. The same special thanks are extended to the young people from each area who spoke candidly about their experiences of the police and their thoughts on cannabis.

We would also like to thank several officers who helped us throughout the lifetime of the study in a number of ways and who always had time to answer our questions: DC Duce, Sergeant Morris, Sergeant Dean, Sergeant Franklin, Inspector Hooton, Inspector Robertson, Inspector Wardle, Inspector Suliaman, Inspector Gutcher, Detective Inspector Bates, Detective Chief Inspector Goulding, Detective Superintendent Roper, Superintendent Southcott and Chief Superintendent Kynnersley.

Many individuals assisted us in the long and arduous task of data collection. Those we would like to thank are: Samantha Carr, Jane Lidgard, Rob Culligan, PC Davis, Inspector Stocker, Inspector Timmins, Detective Inspector Robinson, Detective Chief Inspector Wilkes, Chief Inspector Wisby, Chief Inspector Brown and Detective Inspector Davis.

We are very grateful to several youth workers who provided invaluable assistance and allowed their premises to be used for interviewing: Olive Bowes, Rosie Payne, Cathy Dickinson, Richard Graham, Dawn Orton, Ken Guest, Shokat Khan, Kerry Dean, Jane Wilson, Donna Jones, Hussain Shah, Owen Wright and Mohammed Abdi.

We would also like to thank the Home Office Research Development and Statistics Directorate for allowing us access to the British Crime Survey and the Police National Computer (PNC) dataset. In particular, we would like to thank Philip Howard for his helpful advice and John Corkery for providing us with the national statistics relating to drug offences. We would like to thank the eight Chief Constables who allowed us research access to their forces and supported the study throughout and Maureen Warburton for keeping us up to date with newspaper articles. We would like to extend special thanks to Anna Clancy and Natalie Aye Maung for their assistance with fieldwork and analysis.

Finally, we are very grateful indeed to Advisory Group members Ben Bowling, Mike Goodman, Peter Hampson, Andy Hayman, Roger Howard, Charlie Lloyd, Tim Newburn, Ruth Runciman, Mike Trace, Mark Veljovic, Mike Wilkes and John Witton for their help and support throughout the course of this project.

# Summary

This report describes the findings of a study designed to provide a snapshot of the policing of cannabis in England and Wales. It focuses on the offence of possession. It examines the relationship between policy and practice, how offences of possession come to light, how they are dealt with, and the financial and social consequences of current practice. In part, the study draws on the 2000 British Crime Survey and national police and sentencing statistics for 1999 – the most recent year available – but at its heart are detailed case studies of practice in four police divisions (or basic command units). These involved interviews with police officers and young people, examination of custody records and many hours of observation. The report comes at an important time as changes in the cannabis legislation are likely and, if they occur, approaches to policing will change radically.

Cannabis use is widespread in England and Wales. There are at least three million current users, two million of whom are late teenagers and young adults. Use has grown substantially over the last three decades. However, most use is intermittent, controlled and poses few short-term risks. The cash price of cannabis has been stable for a number of years, so that in real terms prices are much lower than 20 years ago.

As cannabis is a Class B drug, offences of possession carry a maximum penalty of five years' imprisonment, an unlimited fine or both. Prison sentences are actually very rare for possession of cannabis and fines are generally small. However, the five-year maximum sentence makes possession an arrestable offence.

## Enforcement

Many think that the police rarely take formal action against offences involving cannabis. In fact, of the 513,000 known indictable offenders in England and Wales in 1999, just under one in seven (69,377) were cautioned or convicted for possession of cannabis. Since 1989, numbers found guilty or cautioned for cannabis possession rose threefold until they peaked in 1998. They are now falling. Long-run trends in possession offences are available only for the United Kingdom, but these indicate a tenfold increase in possession of cannabis since 1974. These trends are startlingly at odds with trends for all indictable offences, which increased by about a quarter over this period. The most likely explanation for the rapid growth in numbers of possession offences is that the growth in the use of stop and search by the police until the late 1990s interacted with the upward trend in use.

Certainly, we found no evidence that the growth was a consequence of intended policy. None of the police forces in which we undertook our fieldwork had an explicit policy on the policing of cannabis, and none provided specific guidance to its officers about dealing with possession offences. They relied on the guidance issued by the Association of Chief Police Officers (ACPO), which is intended to help decision-making by operational and custody officers. Whilst senior managers were aware of this, we found little evidence that the guidance had penetrated to front-line officers.

## How offences of cannabis possession come to light

Cannabis offences come to light in a variety of ways, which fall into three main groups. They can come to police attention:

- as a by-product of investigation of other offences

- because of obvious and unavoidable evidence of cannabis use

- as part of an intended strategy or tactic targeting cannabis.

### A by-product of other investigations

Possession offences sometimes come to light in the course of an investigation for other offences. The clearest example of this is where a suspect has been arrested for some other offence and, after arrest, is discovered to be in possession of cannabis. For example, suspects may be searched after arrest for offences such as shoplifting and found in possession; sometimes suspects' homes are searched after an arrest and again cannabis is found.

Some police officers suggested to us that this was the most common way for possession offences to come to light. In fact, this turns out to be wrong. Seventy-five per cent of possession arrests in 1999 were for simple possession. The remainder involved concurrent offences, most of which led to the discovery of a possession offence. Analysis of custody records in our four case study sites suggests that the latter may account for about a fifth of all possession arrests.

If only a minority of possession arrests derive from arrests for other offences, they frequently result from stops and searches for other offences which lead only to the discovery of cannabis. In other words, the *specific* suspicion on which the search was based turns out to be unproven or unfounded, but cannabis is discovered in the process. Most of the officers whom we interviewed were of the view that this was the main way cannabis offences came to light.

### Obvious and unavoidable evidence

A second route of discovery is where officers encounter overt cannabis use or obvious evidence of use. For example, officers may see people 'skinning up'(i.e. making a cannabis cigarette); they may see or smell someone smoking a joint in public, or encounter very obvious evidence that they have done so recently. Many officers will feel that, once they have become aware of an offence in this way, they have no option but to take action.

### An intended strategy or tactic targeting cannabis possession

We found no evidence that the level of possession arrests was an intended consequence of a cannabis policing strategy developed at local (basic command unit) level or as part of police force policy. However, it was clear that individual officers sometimes targeted cannabis users, with a view to making arrests for possession.

This happened in a number of ways. Some officers clearly specialise in policing cannabis. In our four case study sites, 11 per cent of officers who had made any arrests for possession accounted for 37 per cent of the arrests; 3 per cent of them accounted for 20 per cent of the arrests. The high arrest rates of some officers may have reflected the nature of the areas in which they worked, but others described how they intentionally pursued cannabis users.

Officers also reported using possession arrests in a more instrumental way, as a 'door opener' to other offences. Analysis of custody records in our case study sites shows that in 8 per cent of cases a cannabis arrest led to the detection of another offence. However, in many cases, this was by accident rather than intent, and the detected offences were almost all relatively minor. Only 1 per cent of arrests for possession led to the discovery of a serious offence involving drug supply, burglary, robbery or firearms.

Stop and search tactics can also be used to impede the activities of a known persistent offender. Almost half of the officers we interviewed reported, at some point in their career, arresting a persistent offender for the possession of cannabis purely to inconvenience them. Prolific burglars or street robbers were often targeted in this way.

Finally, new officers are often encouraged to 'learn the ropes' by making arrests for a variety of offences, including possession offences. Officers reported that cannabis arrests were easy to 'notch up' for probationers, as there was a ready supply of suspects who were likely to be carrying cannabis.

## Case disposals for cannabis possession

Following the discovery of cannabis, the key decisions in the subsequent process are:

- whether to informally warn or arrest the offender

- whether to caution or charge the offender, if arrested

- whether to issue a fine, a court discharge or other sentence, if the offender is prosecuted and convicted.

The policing of cannabis is an area where there is extensive discretion for informal action, even if this is not formally sanctioned by senior officers. We have no way of knowing how many cannabis offences are dealt with informally. Only a third of officers in our case study sites reported that they always arrested those they found in possession of cannabis, with 69 per cent reporting that they had dealt with cannabis informally at some point in their career. Many said they judged each situation on its merits or claimed that they had effectively decriminalised cannabis in their everyday working practices.

A number of factors appear to influence an officer's decision to turn a blind eye. Younger officers or those with short terms of service, those working in more rural areas and those with limited social exposure to cannabis use were more inclined to deal with cannabis formally.

Just over half (58 per cent) of the 69,377[1] known possession offenders in 1999 were cautioned by the police. There were large differences in cautioning rates between police areas. Several factors appear to influence decisions about cautioning or charging including:

- if the offender has a concurrent drug offence

- having other concurrent non-drug offences

- having a previous conviction of any sort.

The remaining 42 per cent were dealt with at court. The most common court disposal was a fine, which was given to six out of ten sentenced offenders. There are large variations across areas in court disposals. Five per cent of those convicted in court were imprisoned for possession; however, the vast majority of these were cases in which the offender was also sentenced to concurrent sentences for other more serious offences.

## Costs and benefits

There are a number of social and financial costs and benefits associated with policing cannabis.

### Social costs

Cannabis use has increasingly become an unexceptional facet of everyday life for young people; this has important implications for the legitimacy of the police. We have seen that possession is one of the offences which is most likely to bring people into 'adversarial' contact with the police. The scope for the erosion of police legitimacy is obvious. If the laws that the police most frequently enforce are regarded by the policed as unreasonable and unnecessary, it is unlikely that police power will be regarded as legitimate.

The young people we spoke with had a range of views about how they were treated by the police when stopped. Some felt that the police were simply doing their job; for them, being treated with respect and receiving a reason for the search seemed to be key factors leading to satisfaction with the encounter. Others felt that the police had been rude or aggressive towards them, that the search was conducted for no apparent reason or that they had been needlessly victimised.

Analysis of the 2000 British Crime Survey (BCS) shows that there are considerable disparities in police-initiated contact between cannabis users and non-users. Cannabis users were nearly twice as likely to report being approached by the police than non-users. A number of studies have found experiencing contact with the police for a cannabis offence is likely to have a negative influence on young people's confidence in the police. We found that there were marked differences in the satisfaction levels of cannabis using and non-using BCS respondents. Fifty-seven per cent of non-cannabis users felt 'fairly treated' compared with only 28 per cent of users. These findings do not amount to proof that the policing of cannabis damages relations between police and young people, but they offer quite powerful circumstantial evidence to this effect.

### Financial costs of policing cannabis

It is difficult to estimate the financial costs of policing cannabis. The police are still in the process of developing unit-based costs for functions such as searching suspects and arresting them, using 'activity-based' costings. We have attempted to estimate the costs of policing cannabis using two methods – neither of which is entirely satisfactory. However, they do suggest the order of magnitude of resources devoted to cannabis offences.

The first uses a Home Office estimate that the cost of policing all drug offences was £516 million in 1999. In that year, there were just under 112,000 recorded drug offences of which 76,769 were for cannabis possession. Using these data, the cost of policing cannabis could be estimated to be £350 million in 1999. This is likely to be an over-estimate.

Our second estimate derives from time actually spent on processing cannabis cases. We found the average time it takes an officer to deal with a cannabis offence was five hours. In most cases officers are operating in pairs. This yields a figure of 770,000 officer hours or the equivalent of 500 officers. A very crude translation of costs into time yields a cost of £500 per case, or £38 million or half a per cent of the police budget per year.

**Possible benefits**

It is difficult to quantify the benefits of policing cannabis. The justification of current practices offered by officers we interviewed included that it:

- reduced the risks that people would use harder drugs

- led to the detection of more serious crime

- helped curb the extent of 'drug driving'.

A lighter enforcement regime is most unlikely to depress usage, but equally it is unlikely to lead to a significant growth in usage. Even if such an increase took place, the best evidence is that an increase in levels of cannabis use would not lead to an increase in the use of more harmful drugs.

While some serious offences are detected as a result of arrests for cannabis possession, our analysis of custody records suggests that this is rare. Our trawl of 30,000 custody records for arrests in our case study areas identified 857

cases where cannabis possession was the primary offence. Out of these 857 cases, 82 led to subsequent arrests for other offences. However, most of these were relatively minor, such as possession of Class A drugs or going equipped to steal. Only 11 out of the 857 cases involved serious crimes of burglary, robbery, drugs supply offences and firearms offences. Furthermore, the discovery of these offences came via a number of routes and some would have been discovered even if the cannabis offence had not been discovered first.

A number of officers raised the inadequacy of drug-driving tests as a reason to oppose reclassification. Our own study can offer no further evidence of direct relevance, but research from Australia suggests that young people regard cannabis as a safe drug for driving. Obviously this issue needs further consideration. Any change to the legalisation needs to be accompanied by a strategy to convey to cannabis users the dangers and consequences of drug driving. It is important that cannabis users understand that use can affect driving and that it can have consequences no less serious than drink driving.

**Costs and benefits of the reclassification of cannabis**

Monetary savings depend on the shape of the new arrangements put into place for disposing of cannabis offenders and the knock-on effects these arrangements have on both levels of informal warnings and stop and search. The savings will be reduced if cumbersome procedures for warning or summonsing offenders substitute for the existing arrest procedures. If streamlined procedures are designed, there could be significant savings. For example, it is questionable whether it is a good use of police time to record possession offences as crimes, as required by the Home Office.

It is perhaps the non-financial benefits of reclassifying cannabis that could have the greatest impact for both the police and the public. Reclassification is likely to remove some of the friction between the police, individuals and communities that currently prevents better and more cooperative relationships.

# 1  Introduction

The cannabis debate has a long history in England and Wales.[1] Since the Misuse of Drugs Act 1971 there have been substantial changes in attitudes towards the drug, in levels of use and in the policing of cannabis. There have been many calls for changes in the law. But there has been no sign of any political will to change – or even review – the legislation until very recently.

The first sign of change was the publication of the Independent Review (Independent Inquiry into the Misuse of Drugs Act 1971, 2000). This advocated that cannabis should be reclassified within the Misuse of Drugs Act 1971 from Class B to Class C. The change would have the effect of reducing maximum sentences for cannabis offences and of removing powers of arrest for possession. The Government initially and very rapidly rejected the recommendation in Spring 2000. The Home Secretary made a formal response to the report six months later, accepting some of the more minor proposals in the report, but rejecting the more central ones such as reclassification. This tough stance appeared to have bipartisan support: at about the same time, the Shadow Home Secretary announced a 'zero tolerance' policy towards cannabis – though this proposal was widely ridiculed.

The policy position of the Association of Chief Police Officers at this time was that it was not pressing for any change in the drugs legislation. However, there was undoubtedly change in the air. In June 2001, the Metropolitan Police announced that it would be running a pilot project in one borough, Lambeth, in which the police would formally warn anyone found in possession of small amounts of cannabis.

During the pilot, there were to be no arrests for offences of possession. In the case of juvenile offenders, the warning was to be treated as an informal one, to ensure that it did not count as a reprimand – one step away from a final warning. At the time of writing, the pilot was being evaluated.

During the 2001 election, support for change came from an unexpected quarter. Several conservative politicians announced that they favoured a review of the drugs legislation, suggesting legalisation of cannabis as an option.

Following the 2001 election, the Parliamentary Home Affairs Committee announced that it proposed to mount an inquiry into the Government's drugs policy. When giving evidence to this inquiry in October 2001, the new Home Secretary announced that he was considering reclassifying cannabis in the way proposed by the Independent Review. He said that he would be seeking advice from the Advisory Council on the Misuse of Drugs (ACMD) with a view to announcing a decision in early 2002. His view was that reclassification would signal a change in priorities for drug policing, and would free police resources to focus on Class A drugs such as heroin and cocaine. At the time of writing, the Home Affairs Committee's inquiry was ongoing, but it had been substantially refocused in the light of the Home Secretary's evidence to it. His final decision had not yet been made. However, no one doubted that there would be some legislative change and many commentators regarded reclassification as a 'done deal'. Thus, for the 'policing of cannabis', times are rapidly changing.

## Background

Cannabis use is widespread in England and Wales. According to the British Crime Survey (BCS), 44 per cent of people aged between 16 and 29 have ever used cannabis, with 22 per cent of this age group using it in 2000 and one in seven (14 per cent) in the month before they were interviewed (Ramsay et al., 2001).[2] There are thus over two million young adults currently using cannabis in the country and approaching 1.5 million using it in the month before interview. Unsurprisingly, use is highest amongst late teenagers and young adults (Graham and Bowling, 1995; Miller and Plant, 1996; Parker et al., 1998; Flood-Page et al., 2000).

The Home Office's Youth Lifestyles Survey (YLS) shows that vulnerable groups such as school truants, those excluded from school, young offenders, homeless young people and those living with drug-using families are more likely than others to use drugs. Of those that used cannabis in the year prior to interview, one in seven did so on a daily basis (Goulden and Sondhi, 2001). A Department of Health (2001) survey found that 12 per cent of children aged 11 to 15 had used cannabis in the previous year, and 28 per cent of 15 year olds had. Williams and Parker (2001) found that seven out of ten 22 year olds in the North West of England had 'ever tried' cannabis.[3]

As a longitudinal study, Parker and colleagues' survey is one of the few sources of information about the development of cannabis use. They tracked roughly 500 young people for eight years from the age of 14. Initially, only three in ten young people had ever tried cannabis. By the age of 18, six in ten young people had done so; by 22, the figure had risen to 70 per cent. However, the survey found some indication that by the age of 22 the proportion of regular ('last month') users was falling off. Twenty-six per cent said they used cannabis in the month before interview, compared with 32 per cent four years earlier.

Information on trends is scarce. Wright and Pearl (1995, quoted in Royal Colleges of Psychiatrists and Physicians, 2000) show a steady increase in the proportion of 14 to 15 year olds offered drugs, from 4 per cent in 1969 to 15 per cent in 1989. There was then a steep increase to 41 per cent in 1994. The BCS offers national trend data which indicate a tripling in 'last year' cannabis use amongst the under-35s from 6 to 7 per cent in the early 1980s to 19 per cent in 2000. However, comparisons are not straightforward as the methodology was consistently improved until 1994 (see Mott and Mirlees-Black, 1995; Ramsay and Partridge, 1999). Since 1994, trends have shown shallow increases.

Most cannabis use is intermittent, controlled and poses few short-term risks to users. The review by the Royal Colleges of Psychiatrists and Physicians (2000) concluded that:

> *Most of those who use cannabis do so without sustaining harm beyond that caused by the toxic effects of cannabis and tobacco smoke on their lungs.*
> (p. 178)

A small proportion of users use cannabis both heavily and persistently; and of these a small proportion present themselves to treatment agencies. Further evidence of heavy and persistent use is evident in Bennett's (2000) survey of the NEW-ADAM programme. Of those arrested ($n$ = 506), 49 per cent tested positive for cannabis. Fifty-nine per cent of arrestees stated that in the 30 days prior to interview they had used cannabis on more than 15 occasions.

### The policing of cannabis

Many think that the police rarely take formal action against offences involving cannabis. In fact, of the 513,000 known indictable offenders in England and Wales in 1999, just under one in seven (69,377) were cautioned or convicted for possession of cannabis. Roughly 10,000 further offenders were convicted of other cannabis offences. Thus, just over one in six known offenders came to police attention in 1999 for offences involving cannabis.

Trends in convictions or cautions for cannabis offences are startlingly at odds with those for other offences. Between 1974 and 1998, numbers in the United Kingdom[4] found guilty or cautioned for any indictable offence rose by a quarter. By contrast, the number of known drug offenders increased more than tenfold, from 11,811 to 129,101. Cases involving possession of cannabis grew from 8,762 to 90,857. This increase in formal enforcement activity probably outstripped the growth in cannabis use in the 1970s and 1980s. It certainly did so in the 1990s.

Policy needs to understand the routes by which cannabis offences are discovered. Whether cannabis offences arise as a result of careful targeting or accidental encounters has important implications for decisions about reclassification and about retaining or removing the power of arrest. There are several possible reasons for the growth in police activity:

- Police policy may have prioritised action against cannabis.

- Performance indicators for drug policing introduced in the early 1990s may have triggered the growth in a less intended way.

- Rising rates of Section 18 searches and PACE (Police and Criminal Evidence Act) searches for non-drug offences may have 'harvested' a growing proportion of drug arrests.

- Arrests for possession of cannabis may be a by-product of the targeting of buyers and sellers of Class A drugs – or an intended form of 'inconvenience policing' (cf. Lee, 1996; Murji,1998).

- A greater prevalence of use and willingness to carry the drug may lead officers to encounter more cannabis offences accidentally.

## Aims and methods of the study

Little research has been carried out on the policing of cannabis legislation. Our knowledge is slight both of current policing practice and of the links between policing policy and practice. This study was intended to go some way to filling the gap. It was commissioned by the Joseph Rowntree Foundation in 2000 to see whether the exponential growth in arrests for possession of cannabis was intended by policy or whether it was a more accidental by-product of low-level police discretion.

The aim of the study was to:

- provide a snapshot view of the policing of cannabis legislation in England and Wales

- trace the relationship between policy and police practice

- assess how this affects individuals and communities.

We designed the study to allow us to mount a multi-level analysis, to yield an overview of the national picture in England and Wales, a more fine-grained account of local practice in eight forces and highly detailed case studies set in two of the eight forces. The eight forces that agreed to take part were:

- Avon and Somerset
- Cleveland
- Metropolitan Police Service
- Nottinghamshire
- South Wales
- South Yorkshire
- Thames Valley
- West Mercia.

The majority of time and effort was spent on the four case studies. These involved 90 observation shifts with operational officers, 150 officer interviews and a manual trawl of just over 30,000 custody records which provided us with detailed information on 1,312 cannabis cases for the year 2000. We also interviewed 61 young people about their experiences of cannabis policing. Full details of the methodology are provided in Appendix 1.

## The structure of the report

Chapter 2 examines cannabis use and cannabis legislation, ending with an examination of recent proposals for change and European approaches to policing cannabis. Chapter 3 describes who comes to the attention of the police and how operational officers enforce the cannabis legislation. Chapter 4 examines police and court disposals for possession offences. Chapter 5 explores the cost of policing cannabis – both social and financial, and, finally, Chapter 6 offers a discussion on the policing of cannabis offences and the impact of reclassifying the drug from Class B to Class C. Appendix 1 provides the full methodology of the study. Appendix 2 outlines the rules that govern police stop and search powers and Appendix 3 provides a glossary of terms used in the report.

# 2 Cannabis use and cannabis policing

This chapter starts with an examination of cannabis use in England and Wales. It then summarises the Misuse of Drugs Act 1971. It explores current police policy in relation to the Act, and describes the recent proposals for change in England and Wales. It then sets out the requirements of United Nations conventions on drugs and describes approaches taken in some other European countries.

## Who uses cannabis?

As discussed in Chapter 1, cannabis use has become widespread in England and Wales, especially amongst young adults. The British Crime Survey (BCS) can offer a profile of cannabis use. In 2000, men were more likely to have used the drug than women, and those aged between 16 and 24 reported greater use than older age groups. Cannabis use was significantly higher amongst people living in London than those living elsewhere. There were differences between ethnic groups, with higher use reported by white and black

people than by Pakistanis and Bangladeshis. Figure 1 shows the percentage of cannabis users (using 'last year') in different social and demographic groups.

We have used the exploratory statistical technique of cluster analysis on the 2000 BCS to develop a fourfold typology of people who say they used cannabis in the last year. We identified the following four broad groups:

1 *Young single hedonists*: predominantly under 30 (all but 7 per cent of the group), single, white, urban. They are usually regular pub goers. Higher proportions go clubbing and drink a lot; this group has the highest proportion of students (20 per cent of the group).

2 *Working class town-dwellers*: predominantly living in urban (not inner-city) locations, most often couples in their mid-twenties or older, higher proportion of low-income households. Quite likely to be regular pub goers, but not heavy drinkers or clubbers.

**Figure 1 Percentage of BCS respondents reporting cannabis use in the previous 12 months**

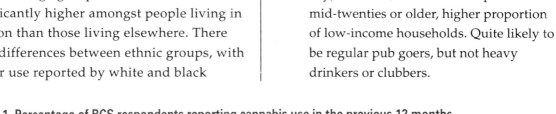

Weighted data, unweighted *n* = 12,593.
Source: 2000 BCS – core sample only.

3   *Affluent metropolitan workers*:
    predominantly aged 25 to 34, tend to be
    in higher income brackets, employed in
    non-manual occupations. More often in a
    relationship, unlikely to drink heavily,
    don't use pubs or clubs much.

4   *Struggling urban men*: in low-income
    occupations, manual workers or
    unemployed, often single, heavy
    drinkers. They don't go pubbing or
    clubbing. Higher proportions of black
    users than Groups 1 to 3.

The analysis illustrates the diversity of
cannabis users. Age is an important defining
variable in the classification; we assume a
developmental process whereby the 'young
single hedonists' will either stop using cannabis
or settle down into one of the other categories.
Young single hedonists and struggling urban
men had the highest levels of regular cannabis
use; 62 per cent and 74 per cent respectively said
that they had used cannabis in the last month.[1]

## The cost of buying cannabis

Most users' expenditure on cannabis will be
modest. Prices have been stable for several
years. Price depends on the quantity and variety
of cannabis. The average UK cost of an ounce is
£90, £100 or £150 dependent on whether it is
herbal, resin, or 'skunk'[2], according to figures
gathered by the police and collated by the
Home Office (2001). The standard cost for an
eighth of an ounce is £15, although 'skunk' is
more expensive.[3] Real-terms prices are lower
than 20 years ago. If prices had risen in line with
inflation since 1980, a £15 deal would now cost
in the region of £37.50.[4]

## The 'normalisation' of cannabis use

Over the years, explanations of drug use have
shifted from subcultural ones designed to
explain the abnormal (Hall and Jefferson, 1976)
to ones that explain why it is that cannabis use
has become an unremarkable feature of
everyday life for large proportions of the
population. Cannabis users are no longer social
'outsiders' (Becker, 1963), nor is cannabis use
demonised as a focus of 'respectable fears'
(Pearson, 1983) in the way it was 30 years ago.
Researchers from Social Policy for Social
Problems Applied Research Centre (SPARC)
explain what they refer to as the 'normalisation'
of drug use by reference to the growth in young
people's economic power, their consequent
growing consumerism and a 'work hard/play
hard' lifestyle which combines risk-taking and
hedonism (Parker *et al.*, 1998; Measham *et al.*,
2000). The researchers suggest that these
lifestyle choices are an understandable reaction
to the uncertainties associated with late
modernity (cf. Giddens, 1991, 1998).[5]

Whilst Parker *et al.* have argued that 'we can
begin to talk about the normalisation of this
kind of drug use' (1998, p.151), some have been
sceptical, deploying survey evidence to show
that drug use remains the exception rather than
the rule (Shiner and Newburn, 1997, 1999). They
have suggested that the concept of
'normalisation' is over-emphasised. We think
that this critique misportrayed the
normalisation thesis as a claim that illicit drug
use is now the norm amongst young people.
Such a claim is demonstrably false. However, it
is clear that cannabis use has lost that set of
social meanings that it had 30 years ago, to do
with social protest, counter-culture and
opposition to the mainstream. It is present in the

fabric of everyday life for most young people, regardless of whether they themselves use it. In relation to young people at least, cannabis use can now be seen as 'part of the definition of a leisure-centred lifestyle' as 'most recreational drug taking takes place as part of a consumer lifestyle, not a deviant one' (Perri 6 *et al.*, 1997, p. 7).

## The Misuse of Drugs Act 1971

The Misuse of Drugs Act 1971 (MDA) was intended to rationalise and draw together into a systematic framework legislation on all psychotropic drugs with a potential for recreational use – excepting, of course, alcohol and nicotine. Under the MDA, all controlled drugs were classified in a three-tiered system. The system was designed to reflect the potential for harm both to the individual and to society posed by the misuse of different drugs. The legislation allows for the Home Secretary to update the list of controlled drugs by amending secondary legislation. The current schedule lists over 200 controlled substances and products.

The purpose of the MDA classification was to ensure that the maximum penalties for different drug offences were in proportion to the risk of individual or social harm posed by the specific drug in question. The Act distinguished between offences of possession and those of supply. At present, Class A drugs carry a maximum penalty of seven years or an unlimited fine for possession, and life imprisonment or an unlimited fine for supply. Offences involving possession of Class B drugs, including cannabis, carry a maximum penalty of five years' imprisonment or an unlimited fine. The maximum penalty for supply of Class B drugs is 14 years or an unlimited fine. Class C

offences carry a maximum of two years for possession and five years for supply.

As we shall see in Chapter 4, prison sentences are rare for possession of cannabis and fines are generally small. The significance of the Class B classification is twofold. First, there is the declaratory impact of classifying the drug as one that carried greater risks than drugs such as steroids and benzodiazepines (both Class C). Second, and of particular importance, the maximum prison sentence was set at a level that makes the possession offence arrestable.[6]

### Trafficking offences, cultivation and allowing premises to be used

The MDA has remained largely unamended since 1971. However, the Drug Trafficking Act 1994 converted supply, possession with intent to supply and production, covered by Sections 4(3), 5(3) and 4(2) respectively, into trafficking offences. The amendments extended courts' sentencing powers for trafficking and included the power to confiscate assets gained from drug sales. Combined with the potential threat of confiscation, trafficking cannabis carries a maximum sentence of 14 years' imprisonment, an unlimited fine or both. A further piece of legislation, the Crime Sentences Act 1997 introduced a mandatory seven-year prison term for a third and any subsequent trafficking offences.

The MDA created an offence relating to the cultivation of cannabis under Section 6. It carries the same maximum sentence of 14 years and/or an unlimited fine as the more serious offence of production. The national statistics make no distinction between production and cultivation of cannabis. This means that there is no clear evidence at national level about the proportion of cultivation offences which are dealt with as production, and thus as a form of trafficking.

Permitting premises to be used for consumption of cannabis is an offence under Section 8 of the MDA, carrying a maximum sentence of 14 years, an unlimited fine or both.

## Policing of cannabis offences: police force policy

As part of the study, we intended to assemble a description of policy on the policing of cannabis in our eight forces. None of the forces had specific guidance on the offence of possession of cannabis, although all had policies and performance indicators relating to the supply of illicit drugs and the possession of Class A drugs.

In 1999, the Association of Chief Police Officers (ACPO, 1999) recognised that case disposals varied among forces, particularly in respect of drug offences, and in response issued guidance aimed at both operational and custody officers to help achieve greater consistency and fairness. However, the guide emphasises that it must not be seen as 'representing authoritative judgements or as obviating the paramount need to consider each case on its own merits'. In relation to cannabis possession, the guidance is intended to help officers decide between the main disposal options:

- formal warning on the street without arrest

- formal warning in the police station

- arrest and caution

- arrest and charge

- arrest and reprimand/final warning (juveniles only).

The guidance is premised on an assessment of case seriousness. Offences committed by adults are placed on a scale of one to five, taking into account a series of aggravating and mitigating factors. For offences scoring five, there is a presumption of prosecution, and for those scoring one a presumption of a formal warning or no further action. A slightly different system has been devised for juvenile offenders, using a four-point scale. This reflects the restricted discretion now available to the police in decisions over the system of reprimands and final warnings for young offenders that replaced formal warnings and cautions.

The guidance stresses that, when making a decision about case disposal, the circumstances and history of the offender are to be considered as well the seriousness of the offence itself. The guidance lists general gravity factors, such as the criminal history of the offender, the likely sentence if prosecuted and the impact of this sentence on the offender. It then goes on to specify the 'entry point' on the scale for each drug offence, and to list specific aggravating and mitigating factors relevant to that offence.

Possession of a controlled Class B drug has an entry point on the scale of three for adults and two for juveniles. Specific aggravating factors for cannabis possession include: large amounts, the offence was committed alongside another offence (for example, theft, burglary, robbery), or the offence was committed by a prison inmate. The only specific mitigating factor was when small amounts of cannabis were involved.

The guidance is silent on what constitutes small and large amounts within the parameters of the possession offence. More surprising, however, was the lack of any indication of the threshold at which possession offences should no longer be dealt with under Section 5(2) but under Section 5(3), possession with intent to supply. This was a cause of frustration for many operational police officers. Several believed that either the Home Office or ACPO should define, at least in general terms, the threshold above which possession is to be treated as possession with intent to supply. They also believed that the threshold should also be agreed in conjunction with the Crown Prosecution Service (CPS), which often provides officers with guidance on criminal charges. There are occasions when CPS advice has been to downgrade a possession with intent to supply to a possession charge when the quantity an individual is arrested with would normally suggest otherwise.

### Scenario

D, a foreign national aged 18, is at an airport awaiting his return flight to his country. In the departure lounge he decides to smoke a 'reefer' cigarette, containing cannabis which he bought while in the United Kingdom. A police officer has cause to speak to D and question him about the cigarette, which he readily admits contains cannabis. The officer examines the cigarette and is satisfied that it does indeed contain cannabis. The officer searches D and his hand luggage (he has no other baggage) with a negative result. D has no previous convictions, cautions or formal warnings.

*Appropriate offence*
Unlawful possession of a Class B drug, i.e. cannabis. Section 5(2) Misuse of Drugs Act 1971.

*Recommendation*
A caution or formal warning is appropriate.

*Mitigating factors*
- No convictions.
- No cautions.
- No formal warnings.
- Likely penalty: a very small or nominal sentence.
- Young offender.

*Supporting notes*
In view of his impending departure from the United Kingdom, his age and the circumstances and nature of the offence, a caution or formal warning is recommended. Given the circumstances, it is unlikely there is a need to arrest D – as such, a formal warning would be the more expeditious disposal. In circumstances similar to these, a formal warning may be administered away from the police station.

*References*
The Code for Crown Prosecutors, June 1994, p. 10, para. 6.5a; p. 12, para. 6.8.

The ACPO guidance provides case scenarios as illustration. Only two relate to cannabis possession. Although the example below is not one that most operational officers will encounter, it does offer some insight into how to dispose of a first-time cannabis offender. As illustrated in the guidance, there can be more than one appropriate disposal.

An interesting element of the guidance is the directive to consider a formal warning. We observed only one inspector in the course of the study who, as a matter of course, used this form of disposal. He rarely arrested and processed first-time cannabis offenders through a custody suite; instead he preferred to formally warn them on the street. He thought that his officers' time should be spent patrolling and being available to respond to emergency calls rather than processing first-time offenders for 'nothing more than a bit of cannabis'.

We did not get a clear sense of whether constables were generally aware that ACPO guidance sanctioned formal warnings on the street. Whatever the case, they generally saw their options as being informal disposal ('down the drain') or arrest. In Chapter 3, we illustrate how operational officers policed the offence of possession of cannabis.

## Recent proposals for change

At the time of writing, debate about cannabis legislation focused around four sets of proposals:

- the Home Secretary's proposal to reclassify cannabis as a Class C drug

- warnings, as in the Lambeth scheme

- decriminalisation

- legalisation.

### Reclassification

This was one of the main recommendations of the Independent Review (Independent Inquiry into the Misuse of Drugs Act 1971, 2000). The legal consequences of this change would be first to reduce the maximum penalty for offences of both possession and supply of cannabis, and second to remove the police powers of arrest. The second change is more far-reaching than the first, because court sentences for possession are already far below the maximum even for Class C drugs.

The Home Secretary could reclassify whilst leaving powers of arrest intact. Legislation has in the past preserved the powers of arrest for a small number of offences, such as taking and driving away a vehicle, criminal damage offences under the value of £2,000 and offences under Section 5 of the Public Order Act (1994), whose maximum sentences would otherwise have made them non-arrestable. However, there would be little point in making a formal change to the law – reclassification – which had no practical effect whatsoever and the Home Secretary's announcement gave a clear indication that the removal of arrest powers lay at the heart of the proposal. Assuming that reclassification removes the power of arrest, the change will significantly alter policing practice:

- Officers discovering small amounts of cannabis will have to decide between proceeding by way of summons, formally warning on the street, informally warning on the street or arresting the suspect under Section 25 of PACE, on the grounds that their identity is inadequately established.

- Formal or informal warnings will probably be organisationally more attractive than the other options.

- Depending on the way these were organised, significant savings of time could be made.

- The arrest rate for Section 1 PACE searches may fall.

- This is likely to affect officers' search practice, reducing the chances of stopping people who are likely to be carrying cannabis but otherwise committing no offence.

- The opportunities for investigating other crimes following arrest for possession will be curtailed.

This decision to reclassify appears to be supported by the general public. A recent ICM opinion poll for *The Guardian* showed that 54 per cent (65 per cent among the 25 to 34 age group) approved of the decision to reclassify cannabis (*Guardian*, 2001).

### Warnings

In June 2001, the Metropolitan Police started a pilot project in one borough, Lambeth, in which the police would formally warn anyone found in possession of small amounts of cannabis.[7] During the pilot there were to be no arrests for offences of possession. In the case of juvenile offenders, the warning was to be treated as an informal one, to ensure that it did not count as a reprimand – one step away from a final warning. At the time of writing the pilot was being evaluated. Although some forces outside of London may follow similar practices, the Lambeth scheme is currently the main example of the practice of issuing formal warnings.

The Lambeth scheme has reportedly been regarded by many as an experiment in decriminalisation if not legalisation. Anecdotally, those upon whom cannabis has been found are puzzled at the fact that the drug

is actually confiscated, because they think it is now legal in Lambeth. In reality, the pilot scheme stops some way short of decriminalisation, a term which is usually used to refer to practice in jurisdictions where possession remains on the statute book as an offence but attracts no enforcement effort at all. Offenders in Lambeth have to admit the offence before they are warned; these are recorded as formal warnings (except for young offenders); and as discussed any cannabis is confiscated.

It is important to recognise that the Lambeth scheme is separate from, and unaffected by, any decision about reclassification. No legislative change was required, as it is well established that the police may issue formal warnings in a number of contexts. (It is debatable, however, whether the informal warning issued to juveniles is in the spirit of the provisions in the Crime and Disorder Act 1998 which allows for only one reprimand and one final warning before offenders are brought to court.) If the pilot proves a success, it will probably be extended to cover the rest of London. At present the warnings are an alternative to arrest. In the event of reclassification, they would simply be an alternative to proceeding by summons.[8]

### Decriminalisation and legalisation

Whilst there is considerable public support for both of these options, neither is likely to get any serious government consideration at least until the reclassification issue has been decided and the new arrangements have had time to bed in. One can envisage a form of 'creeping decriminalisation' whereby warnings become increasingly perfunctory and the criteria for eligibility get stretched.

Certainly, legalisation is a less likely development than decriminalisation, simply because – as discussed in the next section – Britain is a signatory to United Nations conventions which impose an obligation to prohibit the cultivation and supply, though arguably not the possession, of cannabis (Dorn and Jamieson, 2000).

## The United Nations Conventions

The United Nations 1961 Single Convention on Narcotics requires drug misuse and trafficking to be tackled in each country by national legislation. Article 36 suggests that possession of scheduled drugs, which includes cannabis, should attract strong sanctions. The United Nations 1988 Vienna Convention against Illicit Traffic in Narcotic Drugs and Psychotropic Substances states that the possession, purchase or cultivation for personal use of illicit drugs should be criminal offences encompassed under the criminal legislation of each country in the following terms:

> *Subject to its constitutional principles and the basic concepts of its legal system, each Party shall adopt such measures as may be necessary to establish as a criminal offence under its domestic law, when committed intentionally, the possession, purchase or cultivation of narcotic drugs or psychotropic substances for personal consumption.*
> (Article 3, Clause 2)

In amplifying its requirements, however, the Convention further states that countries may differentiate between those drugs that cause the least and the most harm by providing alternatives to criminal sanctions:

> *In appropriate cases of a minor nature, the Parties may provide, as alternatives to conviction or punishment, measures such as education, rehabilitation or social reintegration, as well as, when the offender is a drug abuser, treatment and aftercare.*
> (Article 4:c)

There is thus considerable flexibility in the requirements of the convention. It is clearly within the terms of the convention to retain criminal sanctions for possession, but not to prosecute or punish the offender (Boister, 2001). Dorn and Jamieson (2000) have also pointed towards the possibility of developing civil sanctions alongside criminal ones for minor possession offences. Whilst decriminalisation may well be consistent with the conventions, it is hard to see how legalisation could be so regarded.

## European approaches to cannabis possession

Many European countries are signatories to these conventions and aim to meet their requirements. Increasingly, countries are now implementing legislation or policies in relation to cannabis that are grounded in principles of harm reduction rather than deterrence. Table 1 provides a number of examples, which are intended to be compliant with the United Nations conventions.

Table 1 illustrates the diversity of responses to cannabis possession offences in Europe whilst also highlighting the scope individual countries have when processing offenders. At present, practice in England and Wales is closer to the Swedish approach than to that of most other countries.

**Table 1 European approaches to cannabis possession offences**

| Country | Approach |
| --- | --- |
| Italy | Personal possession is not a criminal offence. Civil sanctions such as the suspension of a driver's licence are, however, applied. Effectively, Italy has 'decriminalised by law'. |
| Netherlands | Possession, selling and growing small amounts are not prosecuted. Small amounts (5g or less) are sold through 'coffee shops'. The Netherlands' approach could be viewed as 'grudging toleration'. |
| Portugal | An individual found in possession of a small amount (not specified) has the drug seized from them and they are referred to a local commission. The commission's remit is to (where possible) divert the individual from prosecution and into treatment. Effectively, Portugal has 'decriminalised by law'. |
| Spain | Personal possession of less than 50g is not a criminal offence. It may attract a civil penalty or a fine. When an individual is caught in possession, the drug is seized and they are referred to the administrative authorities. Effectively, Spain has 'decriminalised by law'. |
| Sweden | No distinction is made between drugs that are considered 'hard' and those considered 'soft'. Usual court sentences are a fine or imprisonment for a maximum of six months. Sweden is widely known for its tough stance against drugs and it would appear that cannabis possession will remain – for the foreseeable future – within the criminal law. |
| Switzerland | Proposed legislation will legalise consumption of cannabis. Only adult Swiss residents will be able to purchase Swiss grown cannabis. The Government is to place greater emphasis on drug prevention policies, and will decide in the near future what quantities and prices will be acceptable. Switzerland – if proposals go ahead – will effectively have 'decriminalised by law'. |
| France | Both simple possession and (uniquely) use are prohibited and punishable by one year's imprisonment and/or 4,000 Euros (£2,500). However, in practice, those found in possession of small amounts receive a warning which is often accompanied by a suggestion (from the police) to attend a social or health service. This process is termed 'no further action with orientation'. |
| Germany | Possession is a criminal offence. However, the Public Prosecutor retains the right not to prosecute where the amount is small and for personal use and it is not in the public interest to prosecute. |

# 3 Enforcement of the law

This chapter examines the enforcement of cannabis legislation in England and Wales, focusing on the offence of possession. Information for this chapter has been derived from Police National Computer (PNC) data, observational work interviews with officers and custody record data. We first examine the volume of cases coming to police attention and the characteristics of offenders. The bulk of the chapter, however, examines how individuals come to police officers' attention.

The PNC database derives from a larger random sample of 30,000 people convicted or cautioned in 1999 in England and Wales. We have assumed that the 2,600 cases involving cannabis possession broadly reflect the totality of cases, but there will be some sampling error in the figures we present.[1]

## People coming to police attention for cannabis possession

There were 76,769 recorded cannabis possession offences in England and Wales during 1999, a rate of 146 offences per 100,000 of the population. Of these offenders, 69,377 were either cautioned or convicted; the shortfall of just over 7,000 is accounted for by cases in which no further action was taken, or the offender was acquitted. Throughout the 1990s, there was a significant growth in cannabis enforcement. Extrapolating from figures for the United Kingdom, there was a threefold increase in the number of possession cases.

This increase was not linear, however. The highest volume of cases was in 1998, when cautions and convictions totalled 77,248. In 1999, they fell to 69,377.[2] There are several possible explanations for this decline:

- the publication of the Macpherson Report (1999) and the criticism it placed on the police for their use of stop and search tactics; Section 1 PACE searches declined by 21 per cent the year after the publication of the report

- the strategic governmental focus on Class A drugs

- a reduction in numbers of uniformed patrol officers

- a greater propensity – due to operational policing pressures – to deal with possession offences *informally*, if at all.

A further drop (16 per cent) in search figures has also been recorded for the year 2000/01, and there has been a further 8 per cent reduction in arrests for drug offences (Home Office, 2001). It would appear, therefore, that the downward trend in cannabis possession offences that began in 1998 is likely to continue into 2002.

### Stop and search

Even if one takes into account the rise of self-reported cannabis use documented by the BCS and other surveys, enforcement activity clearly outstripped the growth in cannabis use during this period. The most likely explanation is that the growth in the use of stop and search powers interacted with a rise in the prevalence of use to produce a surge in numbers of offences until the late 1990s. Certainly, search rates increased sharply over the mid-1990s, whether measured by the BCS or by the Police and Criminal Evidence Act 1984 (PACE) statistics (Home Office, 2001). Though we have no evidence to offer, it also seems likely that, as social acceptability of cannabis use has increased, the rising number of users will have taken less care to conceal cannabis and will have been more prepared to carry it on them in public places. This will have exacerbated the trend.

## Who gets caught for cannabis possession?

The PNC database can provide a good profile of the characteristics of offenders who are cautioned or convicted. The majority of offenders were white males under the age of 25. Only 6 per cent were aged over 40. The imbalance between the sexes should be set beside the BCS findings that gender is a relatively weak predictor of cannabis use. Eight per cent of offenders were black. This is disproportionate to the young black population: around 3 per cent of those aged 16 to 34 are black, according to the Labour Force Survey. The same was true for Asians, but to a much lesser extent; they comprised 5 per cent of arrestees but about 3 per cent of the population aged 16 to 34.

Analysis of 1,312 custody records in our case study areas found similar findings. Only 5 per cent of arrestees were over 40; teenagers between the ages of 17 and 19 comprised a quarter of all arrestees, 92 per cent were male, 20 per cent of those arrested for a cannabis offence were black and 13 per cent Asian. These figures were, however, consistent with the ethnic minority representation in the areas in which we conducted fieldwork.

## How cannabis possession offences come to light

In assessing the operation of the current drugs legislation, and in examining its value, it is important to assess the way in which cases of cannabis come to light. This can happen in several different ways. Cannabis arrests can occur as a by-product of investigation of other offences. It is also not uncommon for patrol officers to fall across cannabis use, for example where people are blatantly smoking it in public, and, finally, the police in some circumstances seek out offences of possession, as part of an intended strategy or tactic.

In the long term, it seems very likely that the balance between these three routes has shifted from the intentional to the accidental. Thirty years ago, the policing of cannabis was largely the responsibility of drug squads; and the policing of cannabis constituted the bulk of these squads' work. With the growth of cannabis use over time, the police have become increasingly likely to encounter cannabis possession as a by-product of other work. Drug squads have also shifted the focus of their work from Class B to Class A drug possession and supply offences, in line with the Government's ten-year strategy.

In the following sections, we provide a snapshot of the ways in which possession offences currently come to light.

## Possession arrests as a by-product of investigation of other offences

Possession offences sometimes come to light in the course of an investigation for other offences. The clearest example of this is where a suspect has been arrested for some other offence, and after arrest is discovered to be in possession of cannabis. For example, suspects may be searched after arrest for offences such as shoplifting and found in possession, or sometimes suspects' homes are searched after an arrest and again cannabis is found. Alternatively, the police may suspect someone of an offence other than cannabis possession, but secure evidence only for the possession offence.

### Possession arrests resulting from arrests for other offences

Some police officers suggested to us that this was the most common way by which possession offences came to light. One of the clearest statements of this particular 'by-product' theory was stated in a letter to us from a police force that decided against participation in the study:

> Perhaps our most fundamental concern [about the study] is that there is no such thing as the 'policing of cannabis' as you state in your letter [requesting access]. The significant majority of offences for cannabis possession are highlighted as a result of arrests for other offences.

Whilst this may have been true in the force in question, it is factually inaccurate for the country as a whole. Our PNC database showed that the majority of arrests (75 per cent) in 1999 were for 'simple possession' with no concurrent offences. As Figure 2 shows, 10 per cent of cases involved other drug offences, such as supply, or possession of Class A drugs and 15 per cent involved other non-drug offences, typically thefts, but no drug offences. (A fifth of the 'other drug' cases or 2 per cent of the total also involved non-drug offences.) It is certainly possible that informal action is taken in relation to much larger numbers of unrecorded possession cases which arise as a result of other arrests – but there still remains a very large number of arrests for simple possession.

**Figure 2 Breakdown of PNC cannabis possession offences by associated crime**

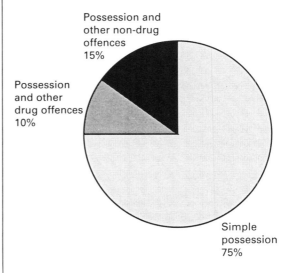

Notes:
PNC data, n = 2,595.
Cases involving both drug and non-drug offences are shown as drug offences.

The PNC data cannot shed any light on the sequencing of concurrent offences. For example, the database cannot tell us whether an arrest for possession led to other enquiries, which resulted in, for example, shoplifting charges, or whether the cannabis offence came to light after an arrest for shoplifting.

Information on the sequencing of possession arrests and those for other concurrent offences can be gleaned only from custody records. To this end, we examined over 30,000 custody records in the four case study areas, from which we found 1,312 cannabis offences; 1,241 of these were cannabis possession offences. In just over a quarter of cases (364), cannabis possession came to light as a result of other offences. In just over a fifth (94) of these cases, the primary offence was another drug offence; and of these 94 cases, over a third (34) were other cannabis offences. It would appear likely that a number of police force areas charge an individual with a possession offence as a 'safety net' charge when the first offence is a supply charge.

**Stop and search – targeting other offences**

If possession arrests are rarely the by-product of arrests for other offences, they frequently result from stops and searches for other offences which lead only to the discovery of cannabis. Most of the officers whom we interviewed were of the view that this was the main way cannabis offences came to light.

The main legislation governing stop and search powers (on foot or in vehicles) is PACE.[3] Officers are required to make a record of any non-voluntary Section 1 searches they carry out, including information about the basis of their suspicion. As the record is made after the event, it is inevitable that there is a degree of convergence between the grounds offered and the outcome recorded.

During the course of our interviews, we asked officers ($n$ = 150) about the last stop and search for drugs they had conducted. Of the total, 133 had mounted such searches. Forty-six were for cannabis and 87 for other drugs. Of the 46 cannabis searches, 20 resulted in the discovery of cannabis. Of the 87 searches for other drugs, 17 had yielded cannabis. Our own sense of the interviews was that, where some respondents unexpectedly discovered cannabis, they were likely to redefine the search as one that was intended to do so. Whatever the case, it is clear that similar numbers of cannabis arrests arose from searches designed to uncover other drugs as did those targeting cannabis.

The following extract from fieldnotes provides one example of a search for Class A drugs that uncovered cannabis. The suspect was alleged to be selling crack-cocaine (crack) from a known open drug market, an offence for which he had been arrested the previous week.

17.30 Officers had information that a known individual was selling crack from his car in a well-known drug market. The suspect had been found in possession of half an ounce of crack the previous week.

The officers spotted the car; the suspect was not there, but two females were in the car. As the marked police car drew up, one of the officers commented that he had seen the female in the passenger seat attempting to hide something. The officers approached the car and asked the two females to get out. They were told they were to be searched on suspicion of possessing drugs. Neither was found to be in possession of a controlled drug. The officers then searched the car. They found a £10 bag of skunk, a wrap of herbal cannabis and three wraps of heroin in the car's ashtray. As a result, both females were arrested on suspicion of possessing controlled substances.

At this point, the suspect arrived. One of the officers asked if he was the owner of the car. After a discussion with one of the officers, he admitted the car was his and that the juvenile was his daughter, and the other female his girlfriend. He was then arrested on suspicion of possessing controlled substances, as he was the owner of the car. All of this took a considerable amount of time – about an hour before the three were taken to a police station.

All three were taken into custody. During the booking-in process both females were strip searched. The male was also found to have £295. This proved further evidence (to the officers) that he was involved in supplying drugs. He was also strip searched for drugs. None of the searches yielded drugs.

20.50 The team inspector sanctioned two Section 18 searches – one at the male detainee's house and one at his girlfriend's. Neither search produced any further drugs.

The suspect was transported to a different station to await the arrival of a CID officer who had dealt with him the previous week. The suspect was then interviewed and admitted to the officers that the drugs were for his own personal use. It was agreed by the officers in the case and the custody sergeant that there was insufficient evidence to substantiate a supply charge. He

was charged with possession of Class A and B drugs (heroin and cannabis). Both females were released without interview or charge at 1.00 a.m. The male was released some time later.

In another example, two officers were patrolling an out-of-town shopping area at 10.00 p.m. where, at that time, it was unusual to see parked cars. The officers saw a stationary vehicle with two young men sitting in it and decided they might be 'up to no good'. On approaching the car one of the officers saw a ripped Rizla packet. Both officers said that the original reason for approaching the car was not suspicion of drug use. However, the resultant search did yield an unintended cannabis detection. The officers asked the young man if he had anything on him that he shouldn't; he produced from his pocket a small amount of cannabis. He was duly arrested. His friend was searched but nothing was found and he was allowed to go home. The arrested lad was 17 and slightly dazed by his arrest stating that it was 'not what I had planned for the night'. The young man was not placed in a cell but was taken directly for an interview.

22.26 Interview commenced. The young lad was asked to explain how he had come to be in a car with cannabis. He stated that he had been driving about with a mate listening to music when they decided to stop for a spliff. They went to a car park and he rolled a spliff; they smoked it outside of the car as the driver's girlfriend does not let anyone smoke anything in the car and they would be 'killed' if she found out. They had just started to get back in the car when the police pulled up. The police approached the vehicle and asked them what they were doing; the young lad stated that he initially just sat there not saying anything, but then noticed that he had dropped – in the front passenger footwell – a cigarette pack and a Rizla paper. The officer asked the young man if he had anything on him that he shouldn't and stated that he intended to search both the car and its occupants for drugs. The young lad had about 2g of skunk on him that he had bought for £10. He told the officers that he had been smoking for about six months and had 'got into it when I was camping with me mates. Someone passed it around, I liked it so carried on buying it.' His mum, dad and gran knew he smoked but he stated, 'if my grandad finds out he will hit the roof'. The officers asked him if he knew the seriousness of supplying drugs to others; he stated that he did and that he would not do it. The interview concluded at 22.37. Both the officers informed the young man that they would recommend to the custody sergeant that he be reprimanded.

The young man was bailed to return to the police station to receive a reprimand in the presence of his mother. We later discovered he had not returned to the police station; one of the officers thought he was probably still too scared to tell his mother of the arrest.

### Inconveniencing persistent offenders

Stop and search can also be used to impede the activities of a known persistent offender. Enforcement activity against persistent offenders enables the police to demonstrate and maintain their authority at a street level. During the course of our formal interviews, we asked 145 officers whether, at some point in their career, they had arrested a persistent offender for the possession of cannabis purely to inconvenience them. Forty-five per cent stated that they had done so. Outside of the formal interview, a number of officers commented that it was prolific burglars or street robbers that were targeted in this way, not, for example, shoplifters.

The following observation details a cannabis offence that originated from a stop and search for an offensive weapon. The arrested individual was well known to the police. He was also believed to have organised an illegal rave that night at which officers thought he might be selling Class A drugs. The arresting officer acknowledged that his decision was guided in part by the desire to inconvenience a persistent offender.

03.28 An immediate response call came through detailing a male in possession of a knife. The only information the officers received was that the suspect was reported to be wearing a blue hooded top and a pair of blue trousers.

Arriving at the location of the alleged incident, both officers spotted a young man who was well known to them, and who they believed had organised an illegal rave that night. One of the officers greeted the young man by his name. The young man was wearing a blue coloured vest and dark trousers. The young man was informed that the police had received a call from a member of the public regarding an individual who was thought to be in possession of a knife. The young man was told he was to be searched on the basis of possibly being in possession of an offensive weapon. The young man stated that he did not carry knives. One of the officers searched him and discovered £5 worth of cannabis resin.

03.40 As a result the young man was arrested. The suspect replied: 'It's not worth arresting me for a bit of puff' and 'Is this the only thing you can get me for?'. At this point, he, his brother and his girlfriend (who had been present during the encounter), become increasingly aggressive and confrontational towards the officers. All three accused the police of harassment. Due to his behaviour, the young man was cuffed and the officers decided to transport him back to the custody suite via a police van. At this point, the young man was placed in the back of the police car whilst the officers waited for the arrival of the van. The detainee became particularly aggressive and started to shout, kick out and punch the headrest of the passenger seat.

05.10 Some time later the suspect was taken for a formal interview. Both officers interviewed the suspect. He chose not to have a solicitor present. He admitted being in possession of the cannabis. The interview lasted four minutes. On completion of the interview, the custody sergeant charged the suspect with possession of a controlled drug. He was bailed and released from custody at 5.38 a.m. The disposal of a caution, given the young man's previous offending history, was not an option open to the custody sergeant.

After the event the arresting officer pointed out that the arrest might have served an additional purpose – the illegal rave, which he was suspected of organising and selling drugs at, may have been brought to an early finish. It was perhaps these two factors that guided the decision-making process to arrest rather than the cannabis per se. Although the officer was partly guided by the knowledge that the individual was a persistent offender, he also stated that he would always arrest someone for cannabis possession as he felt by not doing so he would jeopardise his job. The officer's colleague, however, stated that he would probably have dealt with the situation informally if it had not involved such a well-known local offender.

Targeting individuals who are believed to be actively offending is seen by most officers to be a legitimate police activity. Miller and colleagues (2000) examined to what degree the police targeted individuals because they were 'criminals'. They found that those stopped and searched were more likely to have offended at some point during the previous year. However, slightly over half had not committed any offence aside from the use of drugs (of which 54 per cent used cannabis only). Miller and colleagues (2000) suggest that, when drug use is considered, the use of stop and search appeared more targeted.

In addition to stops on foot, vehicle stops and searches yield a large minority of cannabis possession offences. Data collected from custody records ($n = 1,312$) showed that 16 per cent resulted directly from officers stopping a vehicle. We were unable to ascertain from the records the original reason for the vehicle being stopped. However, during observations, we witnessed a number of vehicle stops that were conducted for a variety of reasons including the following:

- The driver of the vehicle had committed a road traffic offence.

- There were four or five young people in a car that was registered out of the area.

- The driver was not the same gender as the registered keeper (details of which are available to the police).

- The car looked in disrepair.

- A car was being driven late at night by young people. (This was only observed in one of our detailed case study areas.)

The observation below – a vehicle stop – details how a minor traffic offence acted as both a discovery route to a cannabis possession offence whilst simultaneously acting as a useful training tool for a probationer.

### Stop and search as a training exercise – from a minor road traffic offence to a possession arrest

Learning 'the job' is important and can only be done effectively through direct experience. Probationers are encouraged to make a variety of arrests to accumulate experience. During our observation work, a number of officers stated that cannabis arrests were easy to 'notch up' for probationers due to the number of people now carrying the drug. During our interviews, we asked officers if they had arrested an individual to gain experience of a drug arrest whilst a probationer; just over half (80) stated that they had. Although probationers are encouraged to police 'by the rule book', of the 24 probationers we interviewed, ten had disposed of a cannabis offender informally. The cannabis incident below illustrates a probationer's approach to policing cannabis.

This incident occurred during a night shift (22.00 – 06.00). The first part of this case study is based on a conversation with the two officers, the two detainees and entries made in the officers' pocket books. The two detainees confirmed the accuracy of the events.

01.40 Two officers – one a probationer, the other more experienced – stopped a car because the driver was not wearing a seatbelt. The three occupants got out of the car and one of the officers conducted what he described as a 'cursory' search of the vehicle. On the driver's seat he found a small amount of cannabis (about £3 worth). He asked who it belonged to. The driver immediately took responsibility for it. The officers then asked the occupants if there were any other illegal drugs in the car or on their person. One other occupant produced a small amount of cannabis and the driver of the car produced one ecstasy tablet, which he also confirmed was his. The two in possession of drugs were arrested and taken to the station.

01.55 Whilst en route to the police station, the two suspects agreed that the ecstasy tablet should belong to the passenger of the car. The decision was made due to the passenger

already having previous convictions for theft and burglary, and he was also wanted on warrant. The driver had never been in trouble with the police. The suspects informed the police of this on arrival at the station. The officers did not think it was worth arguing about as: 'at least one of them had put their hands up to it'.

The more experienced officer stated that, if the offence had just involved the driver of the car and a small amount of cannabis, he would have taken no further action. The probationer, however, was far keener to arrest and stated that he wanted a drug arrest. He also commented that cannabis is a gateway to other 'harder' drugs such as heroin and crack so the arrest was further justified in his mind.

One of the suspects entered a debate with the probationer regarding the pros and cons of criminalising alcohol and commented:

*How often do you go to a fight and it is caused by puffers? Never. It is always alcohol, am I not right?*
[comment directed to police officer]

The police officer conceded that in most cases he was correct.

Both arrestees thought that the stop and subsequent arrest had been unnecessary and a waste of police time. The driver of the vehicle stated that one of the officers (the probationer) took the whole incident too seriously. He further questioned what harm both he and his friend were doing. One of the officers stated that a warrant was serious so the cannabis arrest was, in his mind, justified.

02.30 After leaving custody, two other officers commented to me that the arrest had been a waste of time. They stated that it was a Saturday night, the shift had received 21 immediate response calls in a two-hour period, it was the busiest night of the week, custody was filling up and several cells were unable to be used, and officer numbers were particularly low. They questioned why the two officers had stopped someone for not wearing a seat belt given the work pressures that night, and concluded that, although one was a probationer and needed the experience, one of them must want to 'join traffic'. They were unsure of how they would have reacted to the ecstasy tablet but commented that they would not have stopped the car in the first place. They continued to joke for some time about the two 'drug barons' in custody.

05.00 The driver of the vehicle was cautioned for possession of cannabis. The passenger was charged with possession of a Class A and B drug and detained due to an outstanding warrant.

## Obvious evidence of cannabis use

A frequent source of cannabis arrests is where officers either see people 'skinning up' (i.e. making a cannabis cigarette) or smoking a joint in public, or they see very obvious evidence that they have done so recently. In such circumstances, there are obvious pressures on the officer to 'do something'. Drug paraphernalia often forms the basis for stops and searches. Suspicion about the influence of drugs (as the basis for a search) derives from three elements: the smell of cannabis (especially in terms of stopped cars), drug paraphernalia (torn cigarette papers, in the case of cannabis, or tinfoil, spoons, etc. for crack or heroin) and general appearance (drunk without the smell of alcohol) (Quinton et al., 2000).

In our fieldwork, we observed several cases, not all of which resulted in arrests. One such example relates to a group of young males who were found in a car park behind a car with a bottle of vodka and a number of Rizla papers scattered around them and the car.

23.30 Officers are assigned to a call regarding criminal damage to a fast food restaurant. The only information available to the officers is that all the lads are Asian and there were a number of them. Considerable damage has been caused. Officers turn into a car park and see three young lads standing behind a car. They approach them and ask what they are up to. Initially, the young men are evasive and somewhat frosty with the two officers, questioning why they have been approached and a group of white lads across the car park hasn't. The officers explain why they are there and why they have stopped the three lads. The atmosphere eases slightly. One of the lads states that he needed the toilet and they wanted some vodka but did not want to share it with their other friends. The officers ask how long they have been there and what they were doing prior to being in the car park.

They then ask about the Rizla papers at their feet. The three suspects deny knowledge of them, stating they had not noticed them until the officers pointed them out. The officers inform the lads that they are to be searched for drugs and ask them if they have ever smoked cannabis. The three deny ever having smoked. One of the officers replies that it is unusual to find lads their age that have not smoked the drug. The three concede to having smoked once at a party but didn't like it. The officers laugh,

as do the three young men. Nothing is found on either the young men or in the car. The officers then inform the driver that it is illegal to drink and drive and warn him not to drink too much vodka. They leave.

## Cannabis possession arrests as part of an intended strategy or tactic

We discussed in Chapter 2 how police force drug policies were generally silent on matters relating to cannabis. Nor did we find any evidence of an explicit strategy for tackling cannabis at Basic Command Unit (BCU) level in our four case study sites. In short, it would be wrong to say that senior or middle managers were in any way directing operational officers to arrest significant numbers of individuals for cannabis possession.

However, it was clear that individual officers sometimes targeted cannabis users, with a view to making arrests for possession. There were two sorts of cases where this occurred:

- where individual officers targeted cannabis possession as an offence which in itself deserved policing

- where possession arrests were made with a view to making further detections.

**Officers specialising in possession offences**
We have clear evidence that some officers specialise in the policing of cannabis. We collected details of arresting officers on the 1,312 custody records relating to cannabis offences that we examined. In total, 666 officers were responsible for 1,312 arrests. However, arrest

rates were very skewed: 11 per cent of the officers accounted for 37 per cent of the arrests; 3 per cent of them accounted for 20 per cent of the arrests. In other words, there was a small number of highly active officers. Ten of them had made over ten arrests each in the previous year, and two had made 22 and 24 arrests each. One of the two held very firm opinions about the 'gateway' theory – that cannabis leads to other more serious drug use – and believed he played an important part in reducing cannabis use in his particular area. This particular officer commented that:

> *It is my duty to operate a zero tolerance attitude towards cannabis ... I have a zero tolerance attitude towards drug use, I'm like a doctor fighting against cancer, I have a professional responsibility to tackle cannabis use.*

Not many of his colleagues shared the same zero tolerance attitude. Although we found little evidence during our observational work of officers targeting cannabis users, during our interviews almost a third (48) of officers stated that a small number of officers within their stations did target the offence.

### Possession as the discovery route to other serious arrestable offences

In some circumstances, the discovery of cannabis itself leads to arrests for more serious offences, and the prospect of further detections can sometimes provide an incentive to take action when offences of possession come to light. It is important to establish the extent to which cannabis possession offences act as a door opener to other offences, in particular serious arrestable offences and those offences that cause greatest public concern. For

Londoners, offences that caused the most concern were burglary, robbery, selling Class A drugs, violence, sexual crime and racial attacks (FitzGerald *et al.*, in press). These public priorities are likely to be similar across the country. If cannabis arrests can be proven to lead to other offences, especially offences that impact on individuals and the community, this has important implications for removing – or not – the power of arrest. The following incident provides an illustration of a cannabis possession arrest acting as a lever to the detection of a more serious arrestable offence.

During our observational fieldwork, an inspector described an incident that had occurred a week earlier. The police had received a report alleging that an individual was selling drugs from a car in the area. Responding to this report, officers located and stopped a vehicle containing three males. During the search, a small amount of cannabis was found underneath the driver's seat. The driver was also found in possession of £500 in cash. A set of scales was found in the vehicle and another male was found in possession of £600. The driver was arrested for possession of cannabis. However, due to the large amount of cash and the presence of a set of scales, the decision to conduct a Section 18 search was taken. The search uncovered £20,000 worth of heroin and £6,000 in cash. During the interview, the suspect admitted to selling an ounce of heroin a day for the last six months, making a claimed profit of between £300,000 and £500,000. If the cannabis had not been found, the officers would not have been able to arrest the individual, even with a large quantity of cash in the vehicle and a set of scales. The value of possession arrests leading to further detections is revisited in Chapter 5 in more detail.

# 4 Case disposals for cannabis possession

This chapter examines case disposals for cannabis possession offences. We have drawn on several sources of data: observational data and interviews with officers; custody record data; the PNC sample of possession cases in 1999; and Home Office sentencing and cautioning statistics. Following the discovery of cannabis, decisions have to be made between:

- informal warning or arrest

- caution or charge, where arrested

- discharge, fine or other sentence, where convicted.

## Informal warning or arrest?

It has often been observed that, unlike many hierarchical bureaucracies, discretion in police forces increases as one moves down the hierarchy (cf. Wilson, 1968). The policing of cannabis is an area where – whatever the rule book may say – there is extensive discretion for informal action.

Just under a third (47) of officers we interviewed in our four sites said that they always arrested those whom they discover in possession of even small amounts of cannabis. As one said:

*Even if I found a bit the size of a pinhead I would nick them.*

Others clearly judged each situation on its relative merits:

*If you stop someone and they are not aggressive or abusive and they don't have a criminal record, I can't see the point in giving them a criminal record for a bit of cannabis.*

Some of the officers we interviewed claimed that they had in effect decriminalised cannabis in their everyday working practices, never arresting anyone for simple possession offences:

*I never nick anyone for cannabis, and never will, unless it's a vanload.*

The observation below is an extract from fieldwork notes describing how two officers decided to use their discretion whilst dealing with two young people who were seen to be 'skinning-up'.

00.30 We respond to an immediate response call about a petrol station that had just been robbed at knife point. The perpetrators had left the scene in a black car.

00.35 Officers I was with decided to search the surrounding area for the car.

00.55 Whilst searching the area for the suspects, the officers spot two males on a wall with their back to the police car. The two young males were rolling what appeared to be a joint. Upon noticing the police, one of the young men threw the cigarette papers and the joint he was 'skinning up' to one side. The officers approached the two and informed them that they had just watched them throw the joint and set of cigarette papers to one side. Both discarded items were found little more than a couple of metres away. The two individuals made no effort to deny that the cannabis belonged to them.

Both individuals were told they were to be searched for drugs; none were found. When asked where the rest of the cannabis was, they stated that was all they had. They backed this up by drawing the officer's attention to an empty bag they had used to carry cannabis on the floor.

The officers proceeded to do checks on both young men; although both had previous convictions to which they had readily admitted to the officers, neither was wanted on warrant. The first had a caution for possessing an offensive weapon, the other a caution for aiding and abetting a theft.

The encounter proceeded in a good-natured manner. The officers informed the two suspects that they would not be arresting them and that no formal action was to follow. Instead they asked one of the suspects to destroy the remaining joint. The suspect stamped on the joint until it was completely unsmokable. Both individuals were then told to go home.

After the event the officers explained the decision-making process that led to the offence being dealt with informally:

- The two were only in possession of one 'joint'.

- Neither denied being in possession of the drug.

- They were honest about their previous criminal convictions.

- They were affable and engaged with the officers in a polite manner.

It was these factors that led the officers to believe that it was not in their, the suspects', or the wider public interest to arrest the two young men. Both officers believed there was little point in 'wasting' six hours at the station processing the suspects for a single joint. If the empty bag had contained additional cannabis, one of the officers stated that: 'they would have been brought in for a caution'. They believed neither individual was causing any harm. However, they said that, if the two individuals had been 'mouthy', then they almost certainly would have been arrested.

Officers during our observation work also commented about discovering cannabis at victims' addresses. We witnessed one such occurrence. The following observation is an extract from fieldwork notes.

03.00 Officers answer a call to a violent domestic. On arrival they discover the domestic is between an estranged wife, and her daughter, with her ex-husband and his new partner. A glass front door had been smashed and all four are in the house hurling abuse at one another. The police quieten the situation down and check that no one is hurt. Advice is given to all parties about

> continuing the situation once they [the police] have left the property. They are informed that if a request is made to return to the address all of them will be arrested. In the kitchen, there is obvious evidence of cannabis use. The officers ignore this and concentrate on the situation they have been called to.

On leaving the property the officers comment about the cannabis paraphernalia and smell in the kitchen, stating that it was just as well the occupants had smoked prior to the ex-wife turning up on the doorstep otherwise 'it really could have got violent'.

During our observational work, a number of officers stated that situations such as the one above had occurred to them. Most officers, in this situation, commented that they used their discretion and generally ignored any evidence of cannabis use. The consensus from officers was that the offence was being committed in a private residence and was not harming anyone but the occupant concerned. It was, as one officer commented, 'pragmatic policing'.

We found that deciding to exercise discretion – with specific regard to cannabis – is not as unusual as other researchers (FitzGerald, 1999) have recently reported. Of the officers we interviewed, 69 per cent had dealt with a cannabis offender informally at some point in their career. Regional variations did, however, exist. In Force A, nearly all (62 of the 76) of the officers we interviewed had at some point dealt informally with a cannabis incident. In Force B, however, fewer officers were inclined to use

their discretion in this way; only 41 of the 74 officers interviewed disclosed informal practices.

Although ACPO stresses to all forces that there should not be 'justice by geography', it would appear that divisions covering more rural areas are less inclined to 'turn a blind eye' to those found in possession of the drug. It is unclear whether officers covering more rural areas encounter harmful substances with the same regularity as inner city policing divisions that cover Class A drug markets. These officers may also consider that cannabis is a harmful or gateway offence and thus do not dispose of it informally. Levels of crime may also have an impact on officers' decisions across areas. Areas that have less recorded crime and fewer immediate response calls may be more inclined to process the offence through the criminal justice system.

We asked our sample of young people ($n = 43$) if they had ever been dealt with informally when found in possession of cannabis. Nineteen had, most of whom had been caught with only a spliff (11) or a very small amount of cannabis. For example:

> *I was with my brother walking along at about midnight. They* [the police] *passed us, stopped us and searched me and found a little bit* [of cannabis]. *They took it from me and asked if my mother knew I smoked. That was it.*

We asked officers whether they had dealt with a cannabis offender informally at any point in their career. Sixty-nine per cent said they had. We asked these officers to describe the last incident and explain what guided their decision-making process. Some of their answers are below:

*I stopped a kid about 14/15 who had a tiny amount of herbal, he was half near to tears about his parents finding out. He had no previous so I dealt with it informally. The shock of being found [in possession] was good enough. The threat of arrest and his parents finding out was explained to him. I deemed it more appropriate to deal with it informally. Also his attitude – he was sorry for what he did.*

*We had been to a burglary and a description was circulated. A male was in the vicinity, we stopped and searched him and found a small piece of cannabis. Another call [a violent domestic] came over the radio. I didn't want to get tied up with cannabis, so we chucked it.*

*It was a group of young people down an alleyway at 3.00 a.m. They discarded a partially smoked spliff [on seeing the police]. It was pointless bringing them in. We gave them advice to do it at home, not on the street. It was not in the public interest [to arrest], and it was a small amount. I don't tend to arrest for a spliff, it's just not worth it.*

Decision-making processes were not automatically guided by what has commonly become known as 'the attitude test'. Many officers, for example, based their decision on the amount of cannabis the offender was found with. Some officers were conscious that they didn't want an offender's first contact with the criminal justice system to be for cannabis. Other officers did not want to leave their colleagues short-staffed on busy nights. One officer commented: 'I would feel dreadful if an urgent assistance came over the radio and I was in custody dealing with a tinpot bit of cannabis whilst one of my shift were getting the shit kicked out of them.' Other officers expressed

similar concerns about the safety of their colleagues.

We examined differences between those of the 150 officers we interviewed who reported dealing with a cannabis offender informally and those who had not. There were small differences in age, with older officers more likely to use informal disposals. Length of service was a better predictor: 76 per cent of those who had served over seven years had used informal disposals compared with 61 per cent of those who had served shorter times. There were even larger differences between the two forces from which the case study sites were drawn: 82 per cent had used informal disposals in one, compared to 41 per cent in the other.

There were also large differences between those who said that they had used cannabis at some stage in their life and those who had not. The sample divided equally into those with and those without experience of the drug – much as one might expect of any sample of adults comprised disproportionately of young men. Eighty-five per cent of those who had experience of cannabis had used informal disposals compared to 53 per cent of those who had not. We ran a logistic regression model to identify the best predictors of use of informal disposals. The most parsimonious model identified length of service, police force area and cannabis use as significant predictors. Having had personal experience of cannabis was the strongest predictor, closely followed by police force area.

In other words, these findings suggest that the chances of getting an informal warning for a possession offence depend partly on the force where the offence is uncovered, partly on the length of experience (and thus, arguably, the professional self-confidence) of the officers involved, and partly on the attitudes of the officers towards cannabis use, which may be mediated by their own experience – or lack of it – of the drug. Certainly, those with experience of cannabis were less likely to regard it as harmful than those who had not. Seventy-four per cent of the former thought that the drug was not very, or not at all harmful, compared with 62 per cent of the latter.

## Caution or charge?

We have no way of knowing how many cannabis possession offences are dealt with informally, but the number of offences recorded by the police is a fairly good guide to the number of arrests. In 1999, there were 76,769 recorded cannabis offences in England and Wales. In 10 per cent (7,392) of these cases, the offenders were never identified, or else they were acquitted or the police decided to take no further action. In 1999, 69,377 offenders were either cautioned or convicted for possession of cannabis.

Nationally, 58 per cent of those arrested for cannabis possession were cautioned. There were large differences between forces. The caution rate for cannabis possession in our eight forces ranged from 40 per cent in Thames Valley to 72 per cent in Avon and Somerset, as Table 2 shows.

There is no simple interpretation of these data. Low arrest rates could indicate either that low priority is attached to this offence, or that cannabis use is lower than elsewhere. A low cautioning rate could indicate a tough policy.

The PNC data show that the outcome of the decision about cautioning or charging was shaped by several factors.[1] If there were any concurrent drug offences, the chances of getting a caution were small: only 18 per cent of such offenders were cautioned. Having other concurrent non-drug offences (e.g. shoplifting) reduced the chances, but to a lesser degree. Having previous convictions of any sort, but especially ones involving drugs, again reduced the chances of a caution. Men were less likely to be cautioned than women, other things being equal.

These factors are cumulative in effect. Thus, some sub-groups were almost certain to be

**Table 2  Cautioning rates for possession in eight forces, 1999**

|  | No. of cases cautioned/convicted | Cases per 100,000 population | % cautioned |
|---|---|---|---|
| Avon and Somerset | 1,333 | 89 | 72 |
| West Mercia | 1,085 | 95 | 67 |
| MPS[a] | 17,324 | 238 | 64 |
| Cleveland | 541 | 97 | 56 |
| South Yorkshire | 1,551 | 119 | 51 |
| Nottinghamshire | 893 | 86 | 49 |
| South Wales | 1,802 | 145 | 46 |
| Thames Valley | 1,484 | 70 | 40 |
| England and Wales 1999 | 69,377 | 132 | 58 |

cautioned and some almost certain to be prosecuted. Ninety-three per cent of first offenders who were arrested for simple possession were cautioned. Almost none of those with both concurrent and previous convictions were.

## Court disposals for cannabis possession

Across all 43 forces in 1999 – a total of 29,386 – 42 per cent of all those cautioned or convicted for cannabis possession offences were dealt with at court. Figure 3 provides a breakdown of disposals for cannabis possession in 1999. The most common court disposal was a fine, accounting for 25 per cent of all cases cautioned or convicted, or six out of ten of those sentenced at court. Eight per cent of all cases, or one in five of those convicted, were given discharges.

There are large variations across areas in court disposals. Amongst our eight forces, fine rates ranged from 42 per cent in Avon and Somerset to 70 per cent in the Metropolitan Police Service (MPS). Imprisonment rates also varied. Nottinghamshire had the highest (10 per cent), while the MPS (2 per cent) imprisoned a much smaller proportion of cases. The PNC data provide a mundane explanation for most of the cases of imprisonment. Three per cent[2] of people on the database (or 8 per cent of those convicted in court) were imprisoned for possession of cannabis. Only six of these 79 cases were ones involving simple possession and only two of these were first offences. The majority of the 79 will have been sentenced to concurrent terms of imprisonment. It is hard to envisage the circumstance, nevertheless, that justified the prison sentences for the two first offenders.

Figure 3  Disposals for cannabis possession offences in 1999

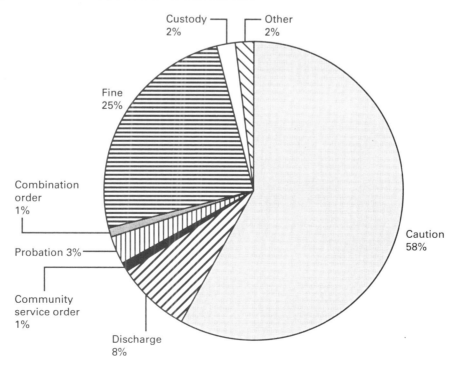

# 5 Dealing with possession: costs and benefits

In this chapter, we consider the costs and benefits of policing cannabis. First, we examine the social cost of current practice including damage to public confidence in the police, and the social and psychological effects of criminalisation of young people. Second, we estimate the financial costs of policing cannabis. Third, we consider the possible benefits accruing to current practice. Finally, we examine the potential financial and social costs and benefits of the reclassification of cannabis.

## Social costs of policing cannabis

In the 1960s and 1970s, the police and the courts regarded possession of cannabis as a much more serious offence than they do now. Offenders could expect to be prosecuted rather than cautioned, and the courts often passed prison sentences. At this time, the policing of cannabis probably enjoyed the confidence and support of the majority of the population, damaging confidence only amongst the relatively small minority of people with experience of cannabis. In Chapter 2, we suggested that over the intervening period cannabis use has become a 'normalised' activity amongst young people. By this we mean not that cannabis use is normal amongst the under-30s, but that its use is now both widespread and unremarkable for this age group, an unexceptional facet of everyday life even amongst those who have never themselves used it. This has important implications for the legitimacy and authority that the police can command amongst young people.

We have seen that, whether by accident or design, cannabis possession is one of the offences that are most likely to bring people into 'adversarial' contact with the police. The scope for erosion of police legitimacy is obvious. If the laws that the police most frequently enforce are regarded by the policed as unreasonable and unnecessary, it is unlikely that police power will be regarded as legitimate. The less legitimacy that the police command amongst young people, the less likely the latter are to accept the authority which the police symbolise. The less authority that the police command, the less they can expect compliance with the law and support for the law. In short, a police force without legitimacy and authority in a democratic society cannot expect to control crime.

What effect does the enforcement of the possession legislation have on relationships between the police and young people? Does it have a damaging effect on police and community relations? Once young people have been charged with possession, what effect does this have on their lives? It is easy to speculate about the answers to these questions, but quite hard to produce firm evidence.

Experiencing a contact for cannabis – or drugs generally – is likely to influence young people's confidence levels in the police. Primarily, such contacts are likely to be the result of a stop and search encounter. Police demeanour has been shown in previous studies to have an impact on levels of satisfaction with the police (Skogan, 1990; Bucke, 1997; Bland et al., 2000a, 2000b; Stone and Pettigrew, 2000). Generally, the experience of being stopped and searched by the police has been found to be commensurate to a decrease in police confidence (Miller et al., 2000). We have tried to shed some light on the issues partly through our interviews with young cannabis users who had been stopped and searched and partly through analysis of the 2000 British Crime Survey.

### Views and experiences of being stopped and searched in our sites

It will be remembered that we interviewed a sample of 61 young people in our four sites. Summing their individual estimates, these respondents had between them been stopped and searched about 500 times. Nearly all had experience of being stopped by the police; numbers of stops ranged from one to 30 times, with a median of five times. Nearly two-thirds reported a stop and search event occurring in the three months before interview. Three-quarters reported that the reason they were usually given when they were stopped by the police was drugs. On the last occasion when our sample of young people were stopped and searched, just over a third (22) were happy with the way they were treated by the police officers. Being treated with respect and receiving a reason for the search seemed key factors leading to satisfaction. Two examples are listed below:

*I was happy because they were not aggressive, and were just doing their job.*

*They explained everything to me, they weren't bossy and they were polite. They were nice about it.*

However, a further third felt the police had been rude or aggressive towards them or that the search was conducted for no apparent reason. The following quotes provide a sense of their reactions:

*I was with my cousin who had just bought some weed and was smoking it. He saw the police and legged it to the park. I didn't run because I hadn't done anything wrong. The police put me up against a wall and started searching me. They were too aggressive.*

*They [the police] roughed us up. They were pushing us around. They rushed over and pushed me against the wall so I couldn't move. I was really scared.*

*I was driving with a friend, they stopped us and told us they could smell cannabis. They stopped us for no reason. They searched us but there was no cannabis and no one had been smoking.*

A further group of 12 interviewees felt victimised because they were already known as cannabis users to the police:

*I'm never happy if an officer just comes up and searches you because it gets tedious if it's every other day. It builds up a bad image and people begin to stereotype you because of your contact with the police.*

We asked them about the effects on their lives of being arrested for possession. Most reported it had not, or would not, have any effect. More than half (37 of the 61 respondents) said that the risk of being stopped and searched by the police did not deter them from buying or carrying cannabis. Those who were concerned about being stopped and searched said that the main thing they feared was having a criminal record. Another common effect (reported by 21) was its impact on family relationships.

*My parents wouldn't trust me as much.*

*It would bring stress to me and my family going to court, having to deal with a solicitor and all that.*

Of the 21 interviewees, 13 were concerned about the effect on their employment chances and a further six linked this to having a criminal record. Six said that for them the most important effect was to make them find alternative methods of transporting cannabis. None of our respondents said that the risk of arrest had any impact on their use of cannabis. Only two mentioned that their attitude to the police changed, as illustrated by the following quote:

*My attitude to the police changed. I had half a spliff and they arrested me. There are people getting murdered just around the corner. We were not doing any harm and they caused a lot of grief.*

**Contact with the police as suspects: the BCS picture**

Obviously, the group of young cannabis users we chose to interview was highly selective, in that nearly all had been stopped and searched and many had been caught possessing cannabis. As described in Chapter 2, the majority of cannabis users will never come to police attention for possession offences. However, the way in which the 61 respondents described their experiences of the police was consistent with findings from the 2000 BCS.

According to the BCS, the police approached 25 per cent of the population aged 16 or over during 1999. Cannabis users were much more likely to be approached than others, as Figure 4 shows. Overall, 45 per cent of cannabis users had been contacted by the police in 1999, which is nearly double the contact rate for the general

**Figure 4 Reasons for police-initiated contact by cannabis use**

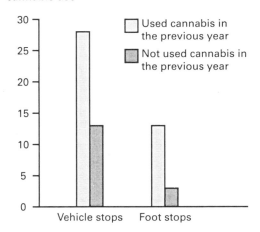

Weighted data, unweighted $n = 6,478$.
Source: 2000 BCS – core sample only.

population. Similarly, more than four times as many cannabis users were stopped on foot and twice as many were stopped in a car compared to non-users, differences that were highly statistically significant ($p < 0.01$).

Figure 4 does not necessarily indicate a causal relationship, of course. The police tend to have more contact with men than with women, and more contact with people under 35 than older people. Those stopped by the police as suspects are very largely men in their late teens and twenties. As this is the group that is also most likely to use cannabis, it is not surprising that there are more users amongst police suspects.

Logistic regression analysis can shed some light on this issue. It can indicate whether possession of one characteristic (in this case cannabis use) is a good predictor of another characteristic (in this case, being stopped by the police) after taking into account other factors (in this case, demographic characteristics such as age, sex and class.) It is a good way of testing out the strength of associations between variables, though it can never itself demonstrate causality beyond doubt.

We conducted logistic regression to identify the best predictors of experience of being stopped by the police. We mounted separate analyses for foot and car stops, testing the following 12 variables for their predictive power: cannabis use in the previous year, age – being aged less than 25, gender, ethnicity (being black, being Pakistani or Bangladeshi, and being Indian) area of residence, social class, income, being a student, car ownership, employment status, educational attainment and patterns of evening activity.

Table 3 ranks variables in descending order of predictive power, excluding all those that failed to be statistically significant predictors ($p > .05$). Both regression models show that cannabis use is a powerful predictor of being stopped both on foot and in a car even when other socio-economic and demographic factors have been taken into account.

What the analysis demonstrates is that cannabis users are not over-represented amongst police suspects simply by virtue of their demographic profile. However, it does not prove that people who use cannabis get stopped more than others simply because they use cannabis. It is possible – if not probable – that people who meet quite separate police criteria of suspiciousness are also more likely than others to use cannabis regularly. Whatever the reasons for the disparity in experience of police stops, it is quite clear that cannabis users are

**Table 3  Variables predicting foot stops and car stops in 1999**

| Foot stops | Car stops |
|---|---|
| 1  Being aged less than 25 | 1  Owning a car |
| 2  Being male | 2  Using cannabis in the previous 12 months |
| 3  Used cannabis in the previous 12 months | 3  Being aged less than 25 |
| 4  Going out after dark more than 3 times per week | 4  Being Pakistani/Bangladeshi |
| 5  Not owning a car | 5  Being male |
| 6  Earning under £15,000 a year | 6  Being black |
|  | 7  Having no academic qualifications |
|  | 8  Going out after dark more than 3 times per week |
|  | 9 Living in London |
| Non-significant variables: education, ethnicity, area of residence, employment status, social class, being a student. | Non-significant variables: being Indian, living in an inner city, income, employment status, social class, being a student. |

Source: 2000 BCS core and booster samples.

much more likely to be stopped and that, if any action arises as a result of the stop, one of the most likely outcomes is an arrest for possession of cannabis.

It will be remembered that ethnic minorities, and black people in particular, were over-represented in cases of cannabis possession. We think it very probable that this over-representation flows at least in part from the over-representation of young black men in stops and in stop and search (cf. Clancy *et al.*, 2001).

**Suspects' ratings of police-initiated contact**
The BCS can give some insights into the impact of experience as a police suspect. Those who had been approached by the police were asked to rate them on politeness, fairness and overall satisfaction with the way the police handled the stop.

Overall, the majority of respondents stopped by the police either on foot or in a car in 1999 felt they had been treated 'very fairly or quite fairly' during the stop. However, there were marked differences in satisfaction between cannabis users and non-users. Fifty-seven per cent of non-cannabis users felt 'very fairly' treated during a foot stop compared to 28 per cent of users. Ratings of police demeanour during car stops were slightly higher amongst both groups although very big differences still persisted, with 38 per cent of users rating the police as 'very fair' compared to 59 per cent of non-users. Differences between users and non-users in perception of police politeness during stops are also marked, with twice as many non-users as users perceiving the police as 'very polite'. Similarly, users reported significantly lower overall satisfaction with the police handling of the stop ($p < 0.01$).

As with the analysis of police contact, these findings do not prove that the users' ratings were lower as a direct or indirect consequence of them being cannabis users. However, they offer circumstantial evidence that cannabis use may be a factor in aggravating relations between police and those – largely young men – who regularly use it.

## Financial costs of policing cannabis

It is difficult to estimate the financial costs of policing cannabis, because the Home Office and the police are still in the process of developing unit costs for functions such as searching suspects and arresting them, using 'activity-based costings'. These are average costs for specified activities, derived from sampling exercising, which measure time spent on the tasks in question. In time, these are likely to provide the best estimates of the financial burden of policing cannabis.

Below we have used two methods to estimate the costs of policing cannabis – neither of which is entirely satisfactory. However, between them, they suggest the order of magnitude of resources devoted to cannabis offences.

**A 'top-down' estimate**
Brand and Price (2000) provided a series of estimates of the costs of various criminal justice activities. We have called this a 'top-down' approach, because they took total expenditure on criminal justice agencies and divided this between different functions, making various assumptions about the relative weight of different parts of agencies' workloads.

Brand and Price put the cost of policing all drug offences at £516 million at 1999 prices. Unfortunately, they did not separate out cannabis offences from others, nor did they distinguish between possession offences and those involving trafficking and supply. Nevertheless, we can calculate a crude unit cost per drug offence, which will provide us with a top estimate for costs in England and Wales:

- In 1999, there were just under 112,000 recorded drug offences (both trafficking and possession).

- The total cost of policing drug offences was £516 million.

- Therefore the cost per drug offence would be £4,605.

- There were 76,769 cannabis possession offences in 1999.

- Cost of policing cannabis in 1999 was £350 million.

As this estimate includes the cost of investigating and prosecuting – more complicated and time-consuming – offences of supply, the figure is bound to be an over-estimate. Whilst cannabis possession accounts for 69 per cent of cases, many of the remaining 31 per cent of cases will have absorbed much more time in investigation and in preparing for trial. The figure of £350 million represents almost 5 per cent of the £7.5 billion police budget in England and Wales in 1999.

### A 'bottom-up' estimate

A lower and probably more realistic estimate can be derived from the time actually spent on processing cannabis cases. We have analysed in detail a sample of custody records for cannabis possession offences in the case study sites. We found that police officers took on average three-and-a-half hours to deal with a cannabis offence from the time of arrest to return to the beat.[1] In most cases, officers are operating in pairs, especially on night shifts (between 22.00 to 06.00) when most cannabis offences are detected. One needs to make a further allowance for time spent on additional tasks done after the offender has been released, and on cautioning offenders or on case preparation in advance of prosecution. In terms of patrol officer time, our findings are fairly consistent with the police evidence presented to the Home Affairs Select Committee on Drugs Policy, that an arrest for cannabis possession absorbs five hours per officer per case. Assuming that officers are working in pairs, this yields a figure of 770,000 officer hours per year – equivalent to around 500 full-time officers.

We should stress that the time taken to process cases varied considerably. Four per cent of cases in the sample of custody records described above took an hour or less from arrest to release, one of which we observed. Similar speed was also reported to us by an inspector who had arrested a young man found in possession of cannabis in Area A. Although he managed to 'jump the queue' to have his arrestee booked in, he still processed the young man from arrest to caution in under an hour. This short length of time for processing individuals is, however, unusual. Whether it could be made the norm rather than the exception is an important issue, but one that falls beyond the scope of this study.

In translating this time into costs, we had a choice between a 'full cost' approach, where we took account of all the relevant policing costs, or a 'marginal cost' approach, where we simply costed the time absorbed by officers to do the work. We thought that a full cost approach was more appropriate, and estimated this very crudely by simply dividing the police budget in 1999/2000 (£7.5 billion) by the number of police constables (100,000). This yields an annual cost per constable of £75,000 and an hourly cost of £50.[2] This 'bottom-up' cost depends on the crude assumption that all supervisory staff and all civil staff work in support of constables, and that all non-staff costs can also be regarded as expenditure in support of constables' work. It yields a unit cost per case of £500, relating to:

- the stop and search

- arrest

- conveying back to the station

- booking in

- repeat search (and possible strip search)

- arrestee placed in a cell

- arresting officer compiles a file and fulfils recording requirements

- taking photograph, DNA sample and fingerprints (if charged or cautioned).

Strictly speaking, this figure should be adjusted downward to take account of the fact that a quarter of cases are processed in parallel with concurrent offences; we have made no allowance for this – but nor have we any reliable means of costing the cautioning process or that of preparing cases for prosecution. We have simply assumed that the savings from handling offences in parallel are offset by the costs of processing cases once the patrol officers have returned to duty.

This yields a total of £38 million in 1999, or half a per cent of the total police budget. There are also costs which fall to the Crown Prosecution Service and the magistrates' courts. Drawing on Home Office Digest 4, the cost of bringing a case to the magistrates' court, from charge to conviction, is £550; there might be further costs associated with sentencing. This would bring the total costs of dealing with cannabis possession up to around £50 million.

Committing 0.5 per cent of the police budget to cases of cannabis possession may look insignificant. However, only around 80 per cent of the constables in England and Wales are engaged on operational duties and, of these, just over half are working on patrol duties. In other words, there are roughly 40,000 patrol officers, and over 1 per cent of their capacity is absorbed in dealing with offences of cannabis possession. Moreover, this effort is not spread evenly across the country. Stops and searches are concentrated in high crime areas, especially in the inner city. As a result, those operational command units with some of the highest crime rates in the country will be spending significant proportions of their budget on the policing of cannabis.

## Possible benefits

Whilst it is hard to arrive at sound estimates of the costs that flow from the policing of the possession of cannabis, it is near impossible to quantify the benefits. However, it is worth examining what these benefits might be. During the course of our interviews and observational work, three sets of justification of current practice were offered by officers:

- By controlling or containing cannabis use, they were reducing the risks that people would use harder (Class A) drugs.

- Through arrests for cannabis possession, they often detected much more serious crimes.

- The illegal nature of possession and the arrestable status of the offence help to curb the extent of 'drug driving' by people intoxicated through cannabis.

**Containing the spread of 'hard drug' usage**

There are two steps to this argument. The first is that current policing practice depresses levels of cannabis use, and the second is that greater cannabis use would lead to greater use of riskier drugs such as heroin and crack.

The argument about the deterrent effects of current practice is hard to test directly. The high prevalence of cannabis use in Britain does not lend much support to the idea. Nor does the fact that usage is lower in some European countries with more tolerant enforcement practice, for example, the Netherlands and Spain (EMCDDA, 2000). However, neither of these arguments is conclusive. It is obvious that at national level consumption of both legal and illegal drugs is determined by many factors beyond enforcement of criminal or administrative law. A lighter enforcement regime in Britain would be most unlikely to depress usage. It might prompt some increase in use, but this is unlikely to be significant (see Ashton, 2001[3] for a discussion).

One can be a little less speculative about the second step in the argument that high levels of cannabis use would lead to higher levels of use of more harmful drugs. There are several variants of

the 'gateway' theory – or 'stepping-stone' theory, as it might more appropriately be called. There is the idea that, after experiencing the mild 'high' of cannabis, people begin to need a more intense 'high' and thus graduate to other drugs. There are equivalent psycho-pharmaceutical arguments that cannabis use triggers the release of chemicals in the brain that increase the desire for drugs. There are arguments rooted in social psychology that cannabis users are more likely than others to come into contact with people with a wider repertoire of drug use, or with people who are keen to sell them other drugs. Versions of these arguments were advanced by one in five of the officers we interviewed. For example:

> As far as I'm concerned it is a drug and if you dabble in cannabis you will dabble in other drugs. It is a slippery slope.

> I feel that cannabis leads onto heavier drugs. Most hard drug users start with cannabis and before you know it you have a heroin addict.

Informed opinion is sceptical about the stepping-stone theory. For example, evidence submitted to the Home Affairs Select Committee on Drugs Policy by DrugScope in 2001 concluded that:

> The theory has proved unsustainable and lacking any real evidence base. The 'evidence' that most heroin users started with cannabis is hardly surprising and demonstrably fails to account for the overwhelmingly vast majority of cannabis users who do not progress to drugs like crack and heroin. The Stepping-Stone theory has been dismissed by scientific inquiry. The notion that cannabis use 'causes' further harmful drug use has been, and should be, comprehensively rejected.
> (Witton, 2001)

The inquiry by the Royal Colleges of Psychiatrists and Physicians (2000) reached similar conclusions, arguing that it was equally plausible that cannabis use might serve as a barrier to use of riskier drugs, or operate as a substitute.

### Detecting more serious crime through arrests for possession

The second argument in favour of retaining the status quo is that arrests for possession lead to the detection of other more serious offences. It is an argument that has been advanced by police officers over a period of years. For example, Monaghan (1991) wrote:

> From the police point of view a 'parking ticket' approach [to cannabis possession] could have major repercussions ... Very often, people arrested in possession of small amounts of cannabis are also engaged in drug trafficking. Many police officers know from experience that the investigation following an arrest for cannabis possession often results in the recovery of more cannabis, other controlled drugs, stolen goods, firearms etc.

The argument was also put forward by police members of the Independent Inquiry (Independent Inquiry into the Misuse of Drugs Act 1971, 2000). There is no doubt that, as discussed in Chapter 3, some serious offences are detected as a result of arrests for cannabis possession. The issue is partly about the frequency with which this happens. Our analysis of custody records suggests that it is rare. Our trawl of 30,000 records identified 857 cases where cannabis possession was the primary offence. In 82 of these cases the arrest was followed by arrest for other offences. The majority of these offences were offensive weapons and possession of Class A drugs. Serious arrestable offences followed in only 11 cases. We have defined 'serious offences' as supply (all classes) and cultivation offences, sexual offences, violent offences, firearms offences, robbery and burglary – those offences routinely highlighted by the public as ones that cause most concern. Of these, three were firearm offences – one of which resulted in a caution; two were Class A supply offences; four involved supply of cannabis offences – all but one resulting in a charge; one was a robbery offence that was transferred to another station; and the final offence was a burglary that was bailed to return and no further information was recorded. The discovery of these offences came via a number of routes and could feasibly have been discovered regardless of the cannabis offence. Two resulted from intelligence passed to the police; one was a public-initiated stop and search; one was a Section 18 search; and the remainder were either vehicle searches or searches of people on foot.

In short, secondary detections arising from arrests for cannabis possession are rare. At least some of these would be foregone if possession were policed more lightly. However, it strikes us that the resources freed up through any such shift of law or practice would be more than sufficient to yield counterbalancing gains in detections. We would also question the principle of retaining an offence on the statute book, or retaining the power of arrest for an offence, purely for the purpose of being able to uncover other offences.

## Drug driving

The issue of drug driving has been relatively submerged in the public debate about cannabis, but it was raised by a number of officers. Although we did not ask directly about drug driving, a number of officers highlighted the present inadequacy of drug driving testing as the reason for opposing reclassification. They felt that current enforcement practice had some value in the absence of effective roadside drug-testing procedures.

Our study can offer no further evidence of direct relevance to this issue, except to flag up its importance. Research from Australia (Lenne *et al.*, 2001) has suggested that young cannabis users perceived cannabis to be a safe drug for driving. Researchers questioned 67 young cannabis users about their views and found that:

*A large proportion of the sample indicated that they perceived cannabis to be a safe drug for driving. These cannabis users do regularly drive while impaired by cannabis, and around half of the sample reported that their cannabis use and driving patterns would not change when proposed changes to the drugs and driving legislation were introduced.*

Although drug-testing measures are being piloted in various police forces, there would also appear to be scope for a government awareness campaign to highlight the dangers and consequences of drug driving. It is important that cannabis users understand that use can affect driving and that it can have consequences no less serious than drink driving.

## Costs and benefits of the reclassification of cannabis

At the time of writing, we were awaiting the Home Secretary's decision about the reclassification of cannabis, and the removal of powers of arrest. What financial savings and other benefits can be anticipated from such a change?

### Financial savings

The cash savings depend, first, on the shape of the new arrangements put into place for disposing of cannabis offenders and, second, on the sort of 'knock-on' effects that these arrangements have on levels of both informal warnings and stop and search. Even if cannabis possession is a non-arrestable Class C offence, it will still come to light, for example in the course of searches. Some arrangements will be needed to dispose of the case, and these arrangements will inevitably have some costs that will offset the savings achieved by not arresting offenders. Some arrangements will also be needed for disposing of confiscated drugs. Different potential elements of the costs are:

- carrying out a search

- issuing a summons

- or alternatively issuing a formal warning

- delivering confiscated drugs to the police station

- recording the discovery of cannabis

- recording the offence.

These processes could be done simply, or they could be done bureaucratically. A key issue will be the extent to which police management feels that it is important to keep a track of the extent of possession offences, which will probably in turn be shaped by the recording requirements imposed by the Home Office. The Lambeth pilot has estimated that the time spent in dealing with possession cases by means of formal warnings was between one and two hours per officer – compared to the five hours currently absorbed by procedures which result in caution or charge.

More important than the unit cost of the new procedure will be its 'knock-on' effects. The downgrading of the possession offence may well have the effect of legitimising informal case disposal. As we saw in the last chapter, informal warnings are commonplace; they could become the norm. In this case the financial savings will be maximised. Alternatively, if police forces decide to proceed by way of formal warning rather than summons, it is possible that the formal warnings may substitute not only for arrest but also for informal warnings. In other words, the provisions could have a sort of 'net-widening' effect. Our best guess is that the declaratory effects of reclassification will in the long term include the extension of informal warnings. In the shorter term, there may well be some net widening, with formal action substituting for informal disposal.

It is possible – if not likely – that the removal of powers of arrest will actually depress overall levels of Section 1 PACE searches. At present, the arrest rate is an important indicator of the efficiency of police use of searches. Removing the power of arrest will remove an incentive to mount a search. This could then lead to the discovery of fewer possession cases, and thus greater financial savings.

### Non-financial benefits

It is perhaps the non-financial benefits of reclassifying cannabis that could have the greatest impact for both the police and public. Although arrests for possession are falling, there are still a considerable number of individuals being processed for the offence who have had no previous contact with the criminal justice system, and possibly will not come into contact with it again. How this damages both the reputation and the legitimacy of the police is difficult to ascertain. As we have seen, contact with the police does not necessarily have a negative impact on young people's views, but cannabis users are less likely to view this contact as 'legitimate'. Our police respondents also echoed this view. Three-quarters (112) of officers felt that the present legislation criminalised individuals who would not otherwise come to the attention of the police, with just under half (74) also believing that the current arrangements damaged their relationship with the communities they policed. In particular, a number of officers (21 per cent) believed that the cannabis legislation affected how young people regarded them, in particular young people from black and Asian communities. Below are a number of quotes illustrating officers' beliefs about the impact of policing cannabis on community–police relationships:

*It affects recreational users, who will develop negative opinions* [if arrested] *when normally they wouldn't come into contact with the police.*

*The young. They feel alienated from us and view us as picking on them when they have done nothing wrong.*

*It* [cannabis legislation] *causes conflict with African-Caribbean, Asian and young people generally. That contact then influences their opinion about the police.*

*It affects youngsters, their experience as youngsters will affect how they view the police later in life. If they get brought in for possession that will give them a negative view and they then won't assist us in serious crimes.*

It will be difficult to assess the impact a change in legislation would have on police and individual or community relations. However, given the perception of the officers we interviewed, it is likely to remove some of the friction that currently prevents better and more cooperative relationships.

# 6  Discussion and conclusions

This report has offered a snapshot of cannabis use and cannabis policing in England and Wales at the turn of the century. Some of its findings are confirmatory, providing evidence for what has been believed or suspected for some time. Other findings, we hope, break new ground. The key points to emerge are as follows.

## Key points

### On cannabis use

- There are at least 3 million cannabis users in England and Wales, 2 million of them under 30.

- Cannabis use has grown over the last two decades and we shall shortly reach a position where the majority of young people have direct experience of the drug.

- The nature of users, and the range of use, is almost as diverse as for alcohol.

- It is clear that overall levels of use for any given age group are rising.

- Most cannabis use is intermittent, controlled and poses few short-term risks to users.

- A small proportion of users use cannabis both heavily and persistently.

- Young men aged 16 to 24 report greater use than older age groups or women.

- Higher use is reported amongst white and black people than Pakistanis and Bangladeshis.

### On policing

- The number of people coming to police attention for cannabis possession increased tenfold between 1974 and 1998.

- Around 2 per cent of users came to police attention in 1999 for possession offences.

- Black people were over-represented in this group.

- Almost two-thirds of those coming to police attention for possession had previous convictions.

- Half of those with previous convictions had no history of drug offences; most of the remainder had previous convictions for both drug offences and non-drug offences.

- Three-quarters of possession offences coming to police attention were unconnected to other offences.

- Ten per cent of cases involved other contemporaneous drug offences and 15 per cent involved other non-drug offences.

- Sixty-one per cent were cautioned and 7 per cent conditionally discharged. Thus two-thirds were not formally punished.

- Twenty-two per cent were fined, 4 per cent given community penalties and 3 per cent given prison sentences – almost always running concurrently with custodial sentences for more serious offences.

- Cautions were usually used for simple possession (73 per cent), but rarely used where there were concurrent offences; in these cases a fine was the most common disposal (30 per cent).

- Eighty-eight per cent of those with no previous cautions or convictions were cautioned, and 93 per cent of those with no previous cautions or convictions and no contemporaneous offences.

- The fivefold increase in possession offences coming to police attention was unplanned and unintended.

- It arose largely as a result of the interaction between increased use of police search powers and increased levels of use (and thus possession).

- Whatever policy is intended, to be workable it must be consistent with the attitudes of officers who have to implement it.

- Most constables favour reform.

- Around half have themselves used cannabis.

### Discovery routes

- Cannabis possession offences come to police attention in a number of ways.

- By far the most frequent discovery route is through stop and search (not necessarily initiated for cannabis or drugs generally).

- Although other more serious offences are uncovered after a cannabis offence, such discoveries are very rare.

- From custody records, just over a fifth of cannabis offences came to light after an arrest/suspicion of another offence.

- On discovery of a cannabis offence there is a disparity in officers' handling of disposals.

### Costs and benefits of police practice

- Cannabis users are more likely than others to be the object of police suspicion.

- This is not simply because of characteristics such as age and sex.

- Cannabis users are much less positive towards the police than others.

- These findings are consistent with, but not proof of, the idea that the way in which cannabis is policed damages police legitimacy amongst this key age group.

- Financial costs are hard to estimate precisely, but cannabis policing probably absorbs the equivalent of 500 constables, or half of 1 per cent of police resources.

- Reclassifying cannabis as a non-arrestable Class C drug would result in some savings, but these could be offset by whatever costs the new arrangements attracted.

- The biggest benefits are likely to be non-financial.

### The impact of reclassifying cannabis

Our analysis suggests that there would be several changes in police practice if cannabis were reclassified to be a Class C drug under the Misuse of Drugs Act, thus losing its status as an arrestable offence.

- Police time could be spent on other more productive activities.

- However, the savings would be significant only in those high crime areas where stop and search tactics are heavily used.

- Levels of stop and search activity would probably fall off.

- Relations between the police and the young working-class males who are typically arrested for possession would improve.

- There might be particular benefits in terms of relations between police and some minority ethnic groups.

- The loss of powers of arrest may result in the loss of a small number of secondary detections which currently arise as a consequence of the cannabis arrest.

- Arrests under Section 25 of PACE (or similar powers under Section 23 of the MDA) would probably increase to compensate for the loss of powers of arrest for possession.

## Putting police time to better use

We have shown that, even though people receive cautions or minor punishments for cannabis possession, police action against these offences absorbs significant resources – perhaps totally half of one per cent of the police budget. Time – and money – is absorbed as a result of the complexity of procedures relating to arrest, disposal of the drug and the statistical recording processes. Reclassification would remove the work associated with the arrest; the resources thereby freed up would depend on what system replaced the existing procedures.

Under the new regime, forces would have to decide whether their normal response to possession would be:

- proceeding by summons
- issuing a formal warning on the street
- issuing a written warning.

How expensive this would be would depend on the complexity of the systems and the weight of the requirements of the recording system. Case for case, there is certainly scope for saving time, but it would be wrong to think that a system of formal warnings is cost-free. A key decision is whether cannabis possession offences need to be recorded as crimes. We cannot see any value in devoting police time to this activity and the Home Office could readily instruct the police to no longer submit returns.

Whatever system replaced the presumption of arrest, there would be a need for a system of disposing of confiscated drugs which protected both against malpractice and against accusations of malpractice. Cumbersome procedures could negate the savings that could otherwise be made. While case-by-case savings may not be substantial, there could be very significant savings if the removal of arrest powers led to a fall in the overall number of searches carried out by the police.

One imponderable is the impact of reclassification on completely informal action. As we have seen, most officers say that they have dealt with cases completely informally. The very demands of the current system may have the effect of driving officers to informal action. The more that reclassification results in a simple, quick and unbureaucratic procedure, the more conceivable it is that there will be 'net widening', with offenders who would have been warned informally now receiving formal or written warnings. It is equally possible, however, that reclassifying will, by signalling lower priority for this offence, result in more completely informal warnings. We think that this is the more likely outcome, unless disproportionate management time is invested in stamping out informal disposals.

## Redeploying the saved resources

One justification advanced for dealing with cannabis possession with a lighter touch is that this would free up resources to address more serious drug problems. Whilst this could happen indirectly, it is unrealistic to think that uniformed patrol officers would shift their focus to Class A drugs and thereby achieve a significant impact on drug problems.

Cannabis use is common; use of heroin and crack remains quite rare. Both use and distribution remain geographically focused in a few places. Except in such places, uniformed patrols would achieve little overall, even if they tried to tackle Class A drug use. Police managers would have two options: the first is to ensure that the freed-up time is put to some other good use by uniformed patrols; the

alternative is to shift resources from patrol strength to specialist units to tackle more serious crime. The latter is the more politically attractive option. However, we think it is important to recognise that the capacity of uniformed patrol officers to respond to day-to-day public demands has already been depleted by many factors including the creation of a multiplicity of specialist units. Our view is that further reductions are simply not viable. Throughout our observational work it was clear how stretched uniformed response teams were.[1] Diverting officers to specialist teams might have the perverse effect of damaging public confidence further.

Expectations about the impact of reclassification should be realistic. In the short term, it is unlikely that the public would notice a visible difference if patrol strength were effectively increased by even as much as 5 per cent. It is unrealistic to expect a short-term reduction in crime figures or an increase in clear-up rates. Freeing up patrol officer time is unlikely to affect crimes that are typically assigned to specialist squads, such as the drug squad, robbery and burglary squad, or CID. However, patrol officers would be freed up to do more of the 'response work' that they currently do – the mucky, unglamorous, often time-consuming work such as stopping pub fights on a Friday night, processing shoplifters, negotiating between neighbour disputes and responding to non-criminal emergencies. We believe that, in the longer term, more responsive policing of this sort will consolidate or regain public confidence in the police and increase police legitimacy.

## Improvements in police–public relations

The main benefits from reclassification may lie less in resource gains and more in improvements in relations between police and public specifically relating to the drug legislation. The searches for drugs and the arrests are a source of friction between police and young people. We have seen that young black people are disproportionately represented amongst these arrests. If the long-term aim of the police is to ensure policing by consent, it makes no sense at all to persist in a practice which damaged their legitimacy amongst the groups whose support they most need.

## Stigmatisation and the curtailing of life opportunities

The impact of an arrest for cannabis possession will obviously vary between groups but the main possible effects, in addition to increased hostility towards the police, are:

- stigmatising or 'labelling' effects

- curtailment of life opportunities, especially employment, as a result of having a criminal record.

The significant minority of offenders with no previous convictions or cautions may suffer both sets of consequences. The more criminally experienced are unlikely to suffer additional problems in getting jobs and may be more impervious to any stigmatising effects. However, they are no less likely to feel resentment at the intrusion into their lives of a piece of criminal law which they regard as unfair and unwarranted.

Reclassification would not in itself change the fact that those who receive a court sentence have acquired a criminal record. However, the likelihood is that the majority of cases dealt with formally will receive only a formal warning, which has no statutory force and which is not recorded centrally. Those receiving formal warnings will not have acquired criminal records. We would thus expect reclassification to have some indirect benefits, particularly on those with no prior record.

## Costs in losing arrest powers

There will be some costs to the police in losing powers of arrest for cannabis possession. Our results show that a small proportion of cases led to the discovery of more serious offending. However, numbers are small: in our custody record analysis, 857 primary offences of cannabis possession led to detections of only 11 serious offences – and even then some of these might have come to light through another route. In weighing up the costs of these lost detections, account must be taken not only of the losses but also of the compensating gains which should result from the savings in police time. It is also worth considering whether it is an acceptable legal principle to retain powers of arrest for an offence simply because it serves as a lever to uncover other more serious offences.

There are some more difficult issues, relating to tactics for the maintenance of police authority on the streets. Popular and political discourse about police work places police officers in a focused 'war on crime'. The reality of patrol work is that a great deal of time is spent negotiating public order. Where patrols are targeting offenders, what they are often doing is letting the offender know that they are around and that they are watching them. In Chapter 3, we have illustrated how the cannabis legislation provides the police with a useful tactic in this process. If known offenders are uncooperative when stopped, they are searched; if they have cannabis on them, they are arrested and charged. The process has a further by-product, serving as an easy way to 'get people on the system' so if they do commit other more serious offences they can be arrested via fingerprints or DNA.

Whether use of arrest in this way is a desirable policing tactic is arguable; that it happens is certain. Many police officers told us that, if and when they loose arrest powers for possession, they will resort to other means for maintaining their authority on those who attract their attention and prove uncooperative. For example, Section 25 of PACE allows officers to arrest for non-arrestable offences where the suspect fails to provide adequate proof of his or her name and address. Another possibility is to use powers to detain suspects under Section 23 of the Misuse of Drugs Act, to enable a strip search to be carried out at the station.

## Warnings and repeat offending

If possession offences are dealt with in the future largely by way of formal warnings on the street, there will be a need for a policy towards repeat offenders. A minority of those coming to police attention for possession will fall into this category. It is hard to see how warnings can be repeatedly issued without the currency becoming totally devalued. A warning which carries no consequences when ignored is no warning at all. One option is to have a 'two strikes' or 'three strikes' system where formal caution or prosecution by way of summons becomes automatic after a specified number of formal warnings. Any such system would need to define the lifespan for these purposes of formal warnings; for example, a formal warning might be regarded as spent, by analogy to the provisions of the 1974 Rehabilitation of Offenders Act, after 12 months.

It will also be important to establish whether or not warnings for cannabis possession given to young offenders count as a reprimand (or in the case of those who had already 'used up' their reprimand, a final warning). If the intention is to minimise the legal consequences of possession offences, there is clearly a strong argument for following the practice of the Lambeth pilot scheme in issuing informal warnings, which do not have the legal status of reprimands and final warnings.

## Deterrence and levels of use

One of the worries often cited by prohibitionists is that, if we relax our cannabis laws and adopt a more liberal stance, a greater number of young people will be encouraged to try the drug, including those who would not have previously tried it due to the deterrent effect provided by the current legislation. It will also be remembered from Chapter 5 that some of the police officers we spoke to had misgivings either about reclassification or about more radical action. They felt that the status of cannabis as a Class B drug and its policing as such ensured that there was a level of deterrent threat. They felt that they were thereby policing the gateway to other forms of more harmful drug use.

There are two questions to consider. The first is whether a relaxation of policing would result in an increase in cannabis use. In Chapter 5, we concluded that a fall in use was improbable and that at least some rise could be expected. The second question is whether this greater use of cannabis would lead to other forms of more serious drug use. There is little evidence in support of the 'stepping-stone' or 'gateway' theory and some evidence against.

In our view, the most plausible stepping-stone will take the shape of cannabis sellers who encourage their customers to broaden their drug repertoire. Thus, the key issue to consider is how a change in policy on possession might interact with drug distribution systems. The tougher the enforcement action against offences of cannabis supply, the more that risk-averse sellers will be deterred. One might speculate that tough enforcement of the cannabis supply legislation will ensure that the retail cannabis market will be run by people who differ little from those who control Class A markets. In other words, if the risk-averse are driven out, the distribution system is likely to be increasingly colonised by criminally involved risk-takers. In our view, the aim of policy on drug supply should be to maximise the separation of the cannabis market system from that of Class A drugs. Precisely how this should be done lies beyond the scope of this report, however.

## Cultivation and supply – choices for policy

Reclassification of cannabis will throw into sharper focus questions about cultivation and

about supply. The first question is whether cultivation – or at least cultivation for personal use – should remain an arrestable offence. There are obvious attractions to the option of creating a new offence of cultivation for personal use and treating it in exactly the same way as possession. Indeed, the ACPO guidelines currently propose that cultivation of small amounts should be treated as possession.

The benefits of this approach would be that, by reducing the risks associated with home cultivation, the latter would thrive. This would then serve as a wedge between users and criminally sophisticated suppliers. Those who relied on home cultivation would have reduced access to more damaging drugs. If arrangements of this sort were to work, it would be important to establish at least indicative guidance as to the threshold between personal and commercial cultivation, probably framed in terms of the maximum number of plants that any individual could grow at any one time without running the risk of arrest.

Greater toleration of possession of cannabis also implies some review of the offence of possession with intent to supply. Where groups collectively purchase cannabis, there is little logic in exposing the one person who is actually holding the drugs to a charge of possession with intent. We think that the law should make some sort of recognition of the issue. This might take the form of a defence in court against a charge of possession with intent, as recommended by the Independent Inquiry (Independent Inquiry into the Misuse of Drugs Act 1971, 2000). We recognise that this would make it yet harder for the police to secure convictions for possession with intent. The officers to whom we talked were almost universally sceptical about the workability of any arrangements which amounted to an offence of 'social supply'; they argued that this would immediately become a standard defence among commercial dealers. But, as the Independent Inquiry argued, failure to recognise the distinction risks bringing the law into disrepute; and the risk will be that much greater if the reclassification of cannabis brings with it an increase in the extent of collective purchasing.

## The law of unintended consequences

Legal and social reform always carries a risk of bringing unintended or even perverse consequences.[2] By way of conclusion, it is worth taking stock of ways in which reclassification of cannabis could backfire.

We have already touched on the first possibility, that reclassification could serve to 'net widen'. If cannabis possession becomes a non-arrestable offence dealt with by a parsimonious system of formal warnings, it is possible that those currently dealt with completely informally may be swept into the new system. Whether this is a desirable outcome needs careful thought. Whether it happens will depend on the signals given by senior police managers to their staff.

The second possibility is that the rank-and-file police may regard reclassification as the 'thin end of the wedge', taking it to signal a relaxation of enforcement for all illicit drugs, including drugs of dependence such as heroin and crack. Policy needs to make it very explicit whether the aim is to achieve a step change in the treatment of all illicit drugs, or to bring about a bifurcation of response which makes a sharper distinction between less risky and more risky drugs. It scarcely needs saying that, in a field as complex as this one, the impact of any legislative changes needs to be charted in close detail.

# Notes

## Summary

1 Excluding those who were acquitted and those against whom the police took no action.

## Chapter 1

1 We have focused on England and Wales throughout this report as other parts of the United Kingdom are covered by different legislation.

2 These figures are likely to be under-estimates, reflecting both sampling and response bias.

3 This higher reporting rate may reflect regional differences, but it is more likely that the trust engendered through participation in several sweeps of a longitudinal survey led to greater openness.

4 Statistics showing long-term trends for England and Wales alone are not available.

## Chapter 2

1 This variable was not included in the cluster analysis.

2 'Skunk' is a hybrid plant specifically bred to produce a very high level of tetrahydrocannabil (THC). The amount of THC determines the strength of the drug.

3 Official price calculations are likely to over-estimate street prices. The baseline figure (one-eighth) is likely to be factored up to provide the costing for an ounce. However, when users buy in larger quantities, the price usually decreases. It is not uncommon to buy an ounce of resin for under £60.

4 Using the ONS deflator for Gross Domestic Product.

5 Giddens has traced the complex linkages between the erosion of traditional certainties about economic, spiritual and family life, ecological threats, the growth of technology, the processes of globalisation, the growth of individualism and, with it, consumerist values.

6 The main legislation defining 'arrestability' is the Police and Criminal Evidence Act 1984; this specifices that offences carrying a five-year maximum sentence are arrestable.

7 Operation Lilac (Metropolitan Police Service) is a Home Office initiative between Camden and Westminster boroughs, and has operated a similar policy to Lambeth for over a year.

8 Another option would be to issue some sort of written warning.

## Chapter 3

1 For example, the true proportion of those cautioned should lie within two percentage points of our estimate of 61 per cent. The national statistics show a figure of 58 per cent.

2 A breakdown of cannabis possession offences for England and Wales was provided by the Home Office.

3 For a summary of the guidance governing reasonable suspicion for stops and searches, see Appendix 2.

## Chapter 4

1  The findings presented here are supported by logistic regression analysis.

2  The difference between this estimate and the 2 per cent in Figure 3 is likely to have arisen through sampling error.

## Chapter 5

1  This timing has been calculated for simple possession offences only.

2  This assumes that officers on average work 200 days a year and that they work 7.5 hours a day, not counting meal breaks.

3  Given in evidence to Home Affairs Select Committee on Drugs Policy by DrugScope. DrugScope is a UK independent centre on drugs. Its aim is to inform policy development and reduce drug-related risk.

## Chapter 6

1  During our observation work, it was noticeable how often operational officers apologised to members of the public for the time it took to respond to their call. Officers quite often attended calls that were over three hours old. One shift started work with 30 outstanding calls.

2  In the field of sentencing reform, for example, measures intended to promote community penalties as an alternative to prison have often attracted relatively minor first offenders.

# Bibliography

ACPO (1999) *A Guide to Case Disposal Options for Drug Offenders*. Cumbria: Cumbria Constabulary

Ashton, M. (2001) 'Legislative frameworks for cannabis', evidence to the Home Affairs Committee Inquiry into Drug Policy, submitted by DrugScope

Becker, H. (1963) *Outsiders: Studies in the Sociology of Deviance*. London: Macmillan

Bennett, T. (2000) *Drugs and Crime: The Results of the Second Developmental Stage of the NEW-ADAM Programme*. Home Office Research Study 205. London: Home Office

Bland, N., Miller, J. and Quinton, P. (2000a) *Upping the PACE? An Evaluation of the Recommendations of the Stephen Lawrence Inquiry on Stops and Searches*. Police Research Series paper 128. London: Home Office

Bland, N., Miller, J. and Quinton, P. (2000b) *Managing the Use and Impact of Searches: A Review of Force Interventions*. Police Research Series 132. London: Home Office

Boister, N. (2001) 'Decriminalising the personal use of cannabis in the United Kingdom: does international law leave room for manoeuvre?', *Criminal Law Review*, pp. 171–83

Brand, S. and Price, R. (2000) *The Economic and Social Costs of Crime*. Home Office Research Study 217. London: Home Office

Bucke, T. (1997) *Ethnicity and Contacts with the Police: Latest Findings from the British Crime Survey*. Home Office Research Study 154. London: Home Office

Clancy, A., Hough, M., Aust, R. and Kershaw, C. (2001) *Crime, Policing and Justice: The Experience of Ethnic Minorities Findings from the 2000 British Crime Survey*. Home Office Research Study 223. London: Home Office.

Corkery, J.M. (2001a) *Drug Seizures and Offender Statistics, United Kingdom, 1999*. London: Home Office

Corkery, J.M. (2001b) *Drug Seizures and Offender Statistics, United Kingdom, 1999: Area Tables*. London: Home Office

Corkery, J.M. (2001c) *Drug Seizures and Offender Statistics, United Kingdom, 1999: Supplementary Tables*. London: Home Office

Department of Health (2001) *Smoking, Drinking and Drug Use among Young People in England 2000*. Available from www.doh.gov.uk

Dorn, N. and Jamieson, A. (2000) *Room for Manoeuvre: Overview of Comparative Legal Research into National Drug Laws of France, Germany, Italy, Spain, the Netherlands and Sweden and their Relation to Three International Drugs Conventions*. London: Institute for the Study of Drug Dependence

EMCDDA (2000) http://eldd.emcdda.org/databases/eldd_cma/comparative_doc/Decriminalisation_Legal_Approaches.pdf

FitzGerald, M. (1999) *Final Report into Stop and Search*. London: Metropolitan Police Service

FitzGerald, M., Joseph, I., Qureshi, T. and Hough, M. (in press) *Policing for London*. Cullompton: Willan Publishing

Flood-Page, C., Campbell, S., Harrington, V. and Millar, J. (2000) *Youth Crime: Findings from the 1998/99 Youth Lifestyles Survey*. Home Office Research Study 145. London: Home Office

Giddens, A. (1991) *Modernity and Self-identity*. Oxford: Polity

Giddens, A. (1998) *The Third Way: The Renewal of Social Democracy*. Cambridge: Polity

Goulden, C. and Sondhi, A. (2001) *At the Margins: Drug Use by Vulnerable Young People in the 1998/99 Youth Lifestyles Survey*. Home Office Research Study 228. London: Home Office

Graham, J. and Bowling, B. (1995) *Young People and Crime*. Home Office Research Study 145. London: Home Office

(*The*) *Guardian* (2001) 'Easing drug laws wins support', 31 October

Hall, S. and Jefferson, T. (eds) (1976) *Resistance through Rituals*. London: Hutchinson

Home Office (2000) *Statistics on Race and the Criminal Justice System: A Home Office Publication under Section 95 of the Criminal Justice Act 1991*. London: Home Office

Home Office (2001) *Arrests for Notifiable Offences and the Operation of Certain Powers under PACE*. London: Home Office

Independent Inquiry into the Misuse of Drugs Act 1971 (2000) *Drugs and the Law*. London: The Police Foundation

Lee, M. (1996) 'London: "community damage limitation" through policing?', in N. Dorn, J. Jepson and E. Savaona (eds) *European Drug Policy and Enforcement*. Basingstoke: Macmillan

Lenne, M.G., Fry, C.L.M., Dietze, P. and Rumbold, G. (2001) 'Attitudes and experiences of people who use cannabis and drive: implications for drugs and driving legislation in Victoria, Australia', *Drugs: Education, Prevention and Policy*, Vol. 8, No. 4, pp. 307–13

Macpherson, W. (1999) *The Stephen Lawrence Inquiry*. Cm. 4262-I. London: The Stationery Office

Measham, F., Parker, H. and Aldridge, J. (2000) *Dancing on Drugs: Risk, Health and Hedonism in the British Club Scene*. London: Free Association Books

Miller, P. and Plant, M. (1996) 'Drinking, smoking and illicit drug use among 15 and 16 year olds in the United Kingdom', *British Medical Journal*, Vol. 313, pp. 394–7

Miller, J., Bland, P. and Quinton, P. (2000) *The Impact of Stops and Searches on Crime and the Community*. Police Research Series paper 127. London: Home Office

Monaghan, G. (1991) 'Powers of arrest for cannabis', *Druglink*, January, p. 15

Mott, J. and Mirlees-Black, C. (1995) *Self-reported Drug Misuse in England and Wales: Findings from the 1992 British Crime Survey*. Research and Planning Unit Paper 89. London: Home Office

Murji, K. (1998) *Policing Drugs*. Aldershot: Ashgate

Parker, H., Aldridge, J. and Measham, F. (1998) *Illegal Leisure: The Normalisation of Adolescent Recreational Drug Use*. London: Routledge

Pearson, G. (1983) *Hooligan: A History of Respectable Fears*. London: Macmillan

Perri 6, Jupp, B., Perry, H. and Laskey, K. (1997) *The Substance of Youth: The Place of Drugs in Young People's Lives Today*. York: Joseph Rowntree Foundation

Quinton, P., Bland, N. and Miller, J. (2000) *Police Stops, Decision-making and Practice*. Police Research Series paper 130. London: Home Office

Ramsay, R. and Partridge, S. (1999) *Drug Misuse Declared in 1998: Results from the British Crime Survey*. Home Office Research Study 197. London: HMSO

Ramsay, M., Baker, P., Goulden, C., Sharp, C. and Sondhi, A. (2001) *Drug Misuse Declared in 2000: Results from the British Crime Survey*. Home Office Research Study 224. London: Home Office

(The) Royal Colleges of Psychiatrists and Physicians (2000) *Drugs: Dilemmas and Choices*. London: Gaskell

Shiner, M. and Newburn, T. (1997) 'Definitely, maybe not? The normalisation of recreational drug use amongst young people', *Sociology*, Vol. 31, No. 3, pp. 511–29

Shiner, M. and Newburn, T. (1999) 'Taking tea with Noel: the place and meaning of drug use in everyday life', in N. South (ed.) *Drugs: Culture, Controls and Everyday Life*. London: Sage

Skogan, W. (1990) *The Police and Public in England and Wales*. Home Office Research Study 117. London: HMSO

Stone, V. and Pettigrew, N. (2000) *The Views of the Public on Stops and Searches*. Police Research Series paper 129. London: Home Office

Williams, L. and Parker, H. (2001) 'Alcohol, cannabis, ecstasy, and cocaine: drugs of reasoned choice amongst young adult recreational drug users in England', *International Journal of Drug Policy*, Vol. 12, Nos 5/6, pp. 397–413

Wilson, J.Q. (1968) *Varieties of Police Behaviour*. Cambridge, MA: Harvard University Press

Witton, J. (2001) 'Cannabis and the gateway hypothesis', evidence to the Home Affairs Committee Inquiry into Drug Policy submitted by DrugScope

Wright, J.D. and Pearl, L. (1995) 'Knowledge and experience of young people aged 14–15 regarding drug misuse, 1969–1994', *British Medical Journal*, Vol. 310, pp. 20–4

# Appendix 1: Methodology

This study involved analysis of national statistics, local statistics and in-depth case studies in two police force areas.

## Analysing official data

At a national level we assembled and synthesised published statistics for England and Wales that related to offences covered by the Misuse of Drugs Act 1971 (MDA 1971). We covered searches and arrests, recorded offences, proceedings (convictions and cautions) and sentencing.

The Home Office provided us with a Police National Computer (PNC) random sample of 30,000 offenders known to have a caution or conviction for any offence in 1998. Of this sample, 10 per cent (2,943) had a caution or a conviction for a cannabis possession offence. We analysed this database to examine the nature of the cases, the way in which they were dealt with, and how this related to contemporaneous offences and criminal history.

Secondary analysis was also carried out on the 2000 British Crime Survey (BCS), to examine people's experience of stop and search and confidence in the police.

### At a local level

We wanted to look at eight police force areas to examine in more detail their policy and practice. In order to select eight force areas we assembled various data. Drug possession figures for all 43 force areas were taken from the 1998 drug seizure and offender statistics published by the Home Office. Using the mid-1999 population estimates, published by the Office of National Statistics, these figures were converted into a rate of cannabis possession per 100,000 of the population. To create a prosecution rate, the proportion of drug offences that received a caution was converted into a percentage for all force areas. Prosecution and drug possession rates were then grouped into low, medium and high categories, thus enabling the creation of a prosecution and drug possession matrix.

We selected police areas that represented:

- low prosecution and high possession rates

- high prosecution and high possession rates

- low prosecution and low possession rates

- high prosecution and low possession rates.

Although the matrix is a fairly crude mechanism for deciding which force areas to concentrate on, it was a useful guidance tool. Such an approach enabled us to make direct comparisons between different policing approaches, between those forces with a low prosecution and high cannabis possession rates and vice versa. The initial selection of force areas, therefore, focused on the corners of the matrix.

In December 2000, we wrote to eight police forces asking for access to detailed statistics for the study. Five agreed and three declined; the three were replaced by other forces. The final eight selected force areas were: Avon and Somerset, Cleveland, Metropolitan Police Service (the Met), Nottinghamshire, South Wales, South Yorkshire, Thames Valley and West Mercia.

Forces were asked to collect information relating to cannabis offences and other drug offences covered under the Misuse of Drugs Act 1971. One of the issues we wanted to explore was what proportion of cannabis offences were secondary offences, i.e. cannabis possession that came to light after an arrest for another offence. We obtained (where possible) detailed statistics on stop and search practice, the arrest rates linked to stop and search, and the outcomes of cases involving possession and possession with intent to supply for cannabis. Analysis examined data on age, gender and ethnicity. Each force was also asked to provide us with force policies relating to cannabis offences to supplement the national guidelines from the Association of Chief Police Officers (ACPO); however, no force had specific guidelines on policing cannabis.

## Four case studies

Two forces (from the eight) were approached and asked if they were prepared to have divisions within their force areas studied in detail. One force declined and we asked another, which accepted. Within each force two specific police divisions were selected. Each pair was selected to contrast in terms of recorded levels of activity against cannabis. Three of the sites were also selected because of the ethnic diversity of their local populations. The four sites have been anonymised in the report to protect their identities.

The four detailed case studies involved:

- observing operational police officers – 45 shifts/90 observations

- interviews with 150 police officers

- analysis of 12 months of data from custody records, for the year 2000

- interviews with 61 young people who had either been stopped and searched or arrested for cannabis offences.

Together these data provide a unique insight into the actual application of the law and its effects.

### Observational work

Observational work was conducted to gain a greater insight into the decision-making processes behind stop and search. Prior to initiating observational work, protocols were drawn up with each force and indemnity agreements signed. We decided to observe one shift in each area. A shift is a set of officers who work together on a permanent basis. This method was preferred, as we were able to build up a level of trust with officers. The researchers recorded details of each shift in note form while out observing officers. Additional material and explanations were added to the notes when the observation sessions were complete.

### Interviews with police officers

Individual interviews were conducted with 150 police officers within the four case study areas. Interviews were semi-structured and covered:

- experiences of policing cannabis

- satisfaction with current enforcement strategies

- decision-making processes when undertaking stop and searches

- experiences and perceptions of the effect of this type of policing activity

- views on this approach and possible alternatives.

### Custody record data collection

Custody record data were collected for the year 2000. This exercise was undertaken in order to get complete data on secondary cannabis offences and the sequencing of cannabis offences. Data collected included:

- demographic information
- how the offence came to light
- time spent in custody
- case disposal(s).

### Interviews with young people

In order to assess the impact of policing cannabis on individuals, we conducted 61 interviews with a sample of 15 to 18 young people per site. They were aged between 11 and 24 years old. Most of the respondents had, in the last two years, been:

- stopped and searched for drugs; or
- arrested for a cannabis offence.

Young people were contacted via local youth groups. Local youth workers assisted us in selecting young people who met our research criteria. In all cases, we met and interviewed young people at their local youth centres.

During the interview process, one interviewee was de-selected as he failed to meet the selection criteria and another was discarded because of the limited number of questions that were answered. The interviews were face to face, combined both structured and semi-structured questions and took approximately 20 minutes to complete. Respondents who took part in the interviews were paid for their time.

## Costing policing cannabis

Finally, we have developed some estimates of the costs of policing cannabis offences, covering:

- a police stop and search that results in no further action

- a police stop and search that results in an arrest

- a police caution or charge for cannabis possession

- the costs of court proceedings.

The methodology for the costing procedure was drawn from cost-effectiveness analysis. Two researchers between January and October 2001 conducted all fieldwork. Although the medicinal use of cannabis is an important issue, it was not in the remit of the study and we have therefore not addressed any of the issues that surround that particular debate.

# Appendix 2: The rules that govern stop and search powers

PACE stipulates that an officer must have reasonable suspicion to search an individual, and this may exist, for example, where:

> ... information has been received such as a description of an article being carried or of a suspected offender: a person acting covertly or warily or attempting to hide something; or a person is carrying a certain type of article at an unusual time or in a place where a number of burglaries or thefts are known to have taken place recently. But the decision to stop and search must be based on all of the facts which bear on the likelihood that an article of a certain kind will be found.

What an officer cannot base their reasonable suspicion on alone is personal factors; for example:

> ...a person's colour, age, hairstyle, or manner of dress, or the fact that he is known to have a previous conviction for possession of an unlawful article, [these factors] cannot be used alone or in combination with each other as the sole basis on which to search that person.

# Appendix 3: Glossary of terms

It is important to develop consistent definitions of terms in this field. In defining decriminalisation and legalisation, we have drawn heavily on the information provided on the European Monitoring Centre for Drugs and Drug Addiction's legal database. We have drawn on the report of the Independent Inquiry into Drugs and the Law (Independent Inquiry into the Misuse of Drugs Act 1971, 2000) for definitions for caution, reprimands, warnings and informal warnings.

## Caution

A caution is a formal warning given by the police. It is not a criminal conviction, but may be cited in court as part of an individual's criminal record. Information about cautions may be given in criminal record certificates (Part V of the Police Act 1997). In certain professions, for example those working with children, employers have the right to apply to the Secretary of State for a record certificate (again covered by the Police Act 1997). There is no provision in the Rehabilitation of Offenders Act 1974 for a caution to be treated as spent. Cautions can only be administered to adult offenders who admit their guilt. A police inspector usually administers a caution in a police station. At present, cautions for recordable offences are kept on the Police National Computer, whilst the remainder are kept locally.

## Decriminalisation

Decriminalisation involves removing the status of criminal law from those acts to which it is applied. This means that in effect these acts no longer constitute criminal offences, though formally they remain on the statute book as crimes. Administrative sanctions may still be applied, such as a fine, suspension of a driving licence, or just a warning.

## Legalisation

Legalisation is the process of bringing within the control of the administrative law a specified activity that was previously illegal and prohibited by the criminal law. Related to drugs, legalisation would mean that activities of consumption and possession, cultivation, production and sale would be regulated by states' norms, in the same way it is legal to use alcohol and tobacco. This means that there can still exist some administrative controls and regulations, which might even be supported by criminal sanctions (e.g. when juveniles or road traffic are concerned). From a legal point of view, any form of legalisation would be contrary to the current UN conventions.

## Reclassification

In this report, reclassification refers to movement of specific drugs from one class to another within the 1971 Misuse of Drugs Act. Here, it usually refers to the transfer of cannabis from Class B to Class C.

## Reprimands and warnings

Reprimands and warnings were introduced in the Crime and Disorder Act 1998 for under-18s. A reprimand is similar to a caution except that repeat reprimands cannot be given; thus, it is not an option for those with previous convictions. A warning results in the offender being referred to a Youth Offending Team (YOT) where an appropriate course of action is decided upon with the aim of diverting a young person away from further contact with the criminal justice system. Warnings, however, may be repeated, but only once (provided two years have passed since the previous warning). Reprimands and warnings can be cited in criminal proceedings.

## Informal warnings

This involves an oral warning sometimes without an arrest taking place. They cannot be cited in court as a part of an offender's criminal record and are often not recorded. Unlike cautions, informal warnings can be administered by constables on the street.